LET THE
DAUGHTERS
THE
Arise

DR. MONIQUE FLEMINGS

For information regarding special discounts for bulk purchases contact the Publisher:
LaBoo Publishing Enterprise, LLC
staff@laboopublishing.com
www.laboopublishing.com

TABLE OF CONTENTS

INTRODUCTION

In a world where women are often seen as second-class citizens, an after-thought, an appendage…it's a necessity to allow the voices of women to rise and be heard. The undeniable timing of the liberation of women from every background and generation must emerge and sound a clarion call. For too long, women have been muzzled and required to sit in the back of the room and be silent. Shame, disappointment and frustration have brewed like a kettle of boiling water within them, longing for the day when they could break their silence. Should they scream? Should they yell? Does it really matter… as long as their voices are allowed to be heard?

As I was preparing to write this book, *Let the Daughters Arise,* I began to pray, which is always my custom in writing. I like to partner with the voice of God as I write and create. As I began to prepare and pray, I heard the voice of the Lord say, "Do not write this one alone." It would have been easy for me to pen my thoughts, but now this project was taking on an incredible life of its own and I was truly up for the journey. My story was not to be a solo project, but to stand with the stories of other women in an authentic anthology of courage, boldness, tenacity, strength, and faith. *Let the Daughters Arise* is a collaboration of powerful women coming together and sharing their battle stories. Within these stories you will find a rich place of wisdom, healing, and practical tools that you can implement in your life immediately. It was our purpose to pen a manual, a legacy piece that represents the power of the voices of women and their fortitude.

One of the greatest examples of women collaborating in the Bible is the example of the daughters of Zelophehad. Each woman was unique and full of purpose. It was when they came together as one mighty tribe that their collaborative voice was powerful enough to shift the culture enough to bring change and create legacy. This is so powerful. They walked in their individualism with their authenticity and collaborated to create lasting change.

Throughout history there are other women who have risen above opposition, sexism, racial injustice, poverty, trauma, self-sabotage, and other roadblocks to stand in their purpose. It has not come without a struggle, a fight, many a shed tear and even days of depression. It has been a journey of pain, self-reflection, low self-esteem and sometimes isolation, but it was worth the journey. The journey was a mentor. The journey was full of purpose.

It is with great honor and intentionality that I share this platform with some amazing women who have co-authored this inaugural anthology, *Let the Daughters Arise*. Each co-author, unique and beautiful, has poured her pain into these pages and shared her ability to stand after the storms of life. This anthology project brought a place of healing for the co-authors as they gave birth to life wisdom.

You will find stories of hope, stories of triumph, stories of shame, stores of fear—you will find pieces of your story woven in these pages. You will laugh, cry, giggle and reach for this book over and over to find strength, knowing that if your sisters overcame you are able to overcome as well.

I invite you...struggling with shame... to ARISE!

Struggling with frustration...ARISE!

Fighting your past mistakes...ARISE!

Thinking it is too late...ARISE!

Betrayed and isolated...ARISE!

Tired of rejection dominating your life...ARISE!

ARISE! ARISE! ARISE!

Let the Daughters Arise!

Let the Daughters Arise in VICTORY!

Let the Daughters Arise in STRENGTH!

Let the Daughters Arise in POWER!

Let the Daughters Arise in WORTH!

Let the Daughters Arise in JOY!

Let the Daughters Arise in PEACE!

Let the Daughters Arise in AUTHENTICITY!

Come on ...I welcome you to ARISE!

Dr. Monique, the Transitions Dr. is the CEO of Monique Flemings Enterprises, a coaching and digital education firm serving faith-based professional women ready to unmuzzle their voice and create a platform for their brilliance. Her diverse background with over three decades as a physical therapist, minister of the gospel and educator, allows her to serve and transform women through a unique, yet practical perspective. Dr. Monique is an international speaker, certified life-coach, five-time author, and six-time co- author, and most was recently featured in the Women of Dignity Magazine.

Dr. Monique is an unapologetic trailblazer for women of this generation and serial entrepreneur that has served as Director of Clinical Education and Adjunct Professor within her profession of Physical Therapy. Along with her other responsibilities, Dr. Flemings serves as the Director of Affiliate Churches for All Nations Collective an urban church planting organization. You can connect with Dr. Monique at moniqueflemings.net

THE DAY MY VOICE WAS MUZZLED

Dr. Monique Flemings

"You sound like you just got off a bus from Mississippi." These words from my high school English teacher were sent to muzzle my voice forever. As an impressionable young lady, I admired my high school teachers. They were the epitome of black excellence. Many of them had graduated from prestigious HBCU (Historical Black Colleges and Universities), and they brought a depth of richness and pride that was undeniable. To walk through the halls and see these pillars of educated black men and women allowed me to set my bar in life high. The sky was the limit. They were my walking heroes who were so close that I could touch them each day. Their wisdom and influence were paramount as community leaders. We were fortunate.

I was struggling with my self-esteem, my identity and even my skin color. Being a light-skinned black girl presented me with a few challenges, and I was failing miserably. In my mind, I was an oddball, strange-looking, and I did not fit in anywhere. I had numerous conversations with my grandmother searching for my identity. I would ask her, "Who do I look like in this family?" What I was really saying was "I feel like I don't fit in…anywhere."

In her effort to bring me peace and resolution, she would pull out pictures of my family members and try to show me where I resembled them when they were younger. It was a temporary bandage. My soul was bleeding. Her comfort would last a moment, then the feelings would come back with a vengeance.

Growing up I was familiar with the childhood chant "Sticks and stones may break my bones, but words will never hurt me." This was to suggest that words could not cause physical pain and I could ignore what people said about me. However, this was far from the truth. It was hurtful words that had penetrated my soul and set up residence within me and were gathering more ammunition to war against me. Words are powerful and words were—and are—able to inflict pain.

When my high school English teacher made a statement to me, it muzzled my voice. It was a public speaking class and just after I gave my speech, she looked at me and made this horrendous statement. She continued to say that I had a horrible Mississippi dialect. It numbed me at that moment, and I did my best to keep a straight face, but it was clear that she was tearing me down with her words. It was not a statement to build or encourage me, but it was a word to destroy me. In a few seconds her words ripped away everything that I was being trained for as a public speaker and as a woman.

I was not new to public speaking. My mother had placed me in every church event that was available for public speaking since I was seven years old. I spoke in various settings and was being training to speak publicly. Like anyone I would get a bit nervous, but once I got started it was on and poppin'! This high school class was to assist me in my further development as a public speaker. In a few seconds, my voice was muzzled by these damaging words from this teacher. I would struggle for years afterward with speaking in my authentic voice. Now this goes beyond the actual art of speaking but penetrates my deeper feelings of worth and value. This was an assault on my presence, my voice, my influence.

That was the day that muzzle came to destroy my voice.

The Cut was Deep

What happened in that moment muzzled my appreciation and love for how I spoke and how I sounded. It was a crushing of my authenticity and what made me uniquely me. My sound was unacceptable was the message that was coded in my mind. My sound was not effective, and my sound was not enough. My public speaking was now tainted and inauthentic. I spent years trying to sound different and not sound like I was from Mississippi. Now, no disrespect to anyone from Mississippi. This was confusing to me because my dad was born in Mississippi, and I have family that live in Mississippi. My Big Momma lived in Mississippi. The questions arose about all of this in that brief second. "What is wrong with Mississippi and what is wrong with me?"

For the next years I would hear this teacher's crushing statement every time I spoke. Can you imagine the turmoil of the inner conflict that was occurring? While others enjoyed my speaking and later preaching voice, I was silently battling a personal war with a statement that was pinned on me at the age of 16. It would be a mental struggle for years as I spoke. I tried to change how I sounded. I continued with public speaking classes and theatre in college and silently struggled with how I sounded to myself. This struggle made me second-guess my significance in every place my voice was required.

Speaking was a part of my life. It was a part of my DNA, but there had been an assault on this gift. If you observe a child playing, they will usually play and express their natural gifts and talents. One of my natural gifts is the gift of speaking and expression. I was always talking in school and often getting in trouble because I always had something to say. I also liked role playing as the teacher in school, or the preacher, which was odd because I did not see very many women preachers as a young child, but this was my normal role play. I was born to speak.

I can recall preaching an immensely powerful sermon where many people were impacted by the message that was delivered. It was an honor to see God's people receive what they needed from God, and it was an honor to be His vessel. But this vessel was broken in many places. This vessel was uncomfortable with my sound, my tone, my dialect….my authenticity. I was uncomfortable in what made me uniquely me. I was struggling even in receiving feedback because of what was happening in my head. I could not listen to myself speak or preach because all I heard was this damaging statement over and over. The negative report had set up residence and was alive and well in my thought processes.

Have you ever struggled silently? Have you ever thought negatively about yourself regardless of what was going on, good or bad, around you? Have you ever smiled knowing that you were struggling, and a muzzle was on the authentic you? Have you ever struggled with a spoken word that crushed you at your very core?

If you answered yes, I believe that these next few pages will bring life to your circumstance. Understand that I had a relationship with God since the age of seven. I understood Him at the point of salvation, but I would soon encounter Him as healer of my damaged soul.

As my life progressed and many opportunities opened for me in my career and in ministry there was always a voice in my head reminding me that my voice was unacceptable. This inner voice was strong and full of judgment. This muzzle became a part of my life and everywhere I went this muzzle was with me, completing its job description to keep me silent and in shame. When I graduated from physical therapy school, the muzzle was present. When I received my license to preach the gospel, this muzzle was present. When my career advanced, the muzzle advanced with me. The muzzle was present and accounted for to keep me silent, and not authentic. The muzzle kept me feeling like my words did not matter, my voice did not matter.

Because the muzzle was with me for so long, I became comfortable with the inner struggle. But one day the inner struggle became too much. It was a long time coming but that day of freedom finally came. But it required participation from me because I had given this muzzle more power in my life than it should have ever had. It was time to remove the muzzle.

Removing the muzzle

1. **<u>Recognizing that the damage was sent to destroy me.</u>** It was necessary to see this experience as a threat to my life and purpose and not just a little mistake from the teacher. For years I felt maybe I overreacted to the situation, and it was not that bad. However, that was not the truth. This experience had a goal to destroy me. Recognizing it allows me to place it in the proper perspective and not gloss over it as if it did not create a tremendous crushing in my soul. Because I failed to recognize this experience as an enemy, I

found myself repeating this experience over and over again because my brain did not recognize it as toxic to my destiny. I welcomed these experiences and each time they were toxic. When I recognized that this original experience was sent to destroy me and I welcomed the additional experiences because I had not set proper boundaries, I soon began to recognize when experiences were sent to destroy me. Recognize your experiences and label them accordingly.

2. **I am not responsible for the opinions of others.** What was spoken was that teacher's opinion and not the truth about me. People, even people of influence, can say many things about you. That is their opinion, and their opinion does not mean that it's the truth. This was difficult because I wanted people's opinions of me to line up with the truth about me, and the two are not always the same. I especially wanted opinions of influential people to welcome me and validate me. Freedom began when I recognized the two are not the same and I am not responsible for the opinions of others. Additionally, I cannot be attached to what others think about me because I will always be trying to live my life according to their standards. This teacher was an English teacher, but she was not the captain of my destiny. She was not the person who would open the door to my next step in life. I fumbled a lot in life because I searched for the opinions of others to be my truth. The truth of who I am is not based on the opinions of others.

3. **Build a healthy self-esteem.** The muzzle over my voice could only exist because my perception welcomed the negative. My cup of good self-esteem was low. The muzzle had a great opportunity to hold me hostage against my

authentic self because my cup of low self-esteem was present and welcomed it. Building a healthy self-esteem meant that I needed to fill my cup with what God says about me. What are the promises over my life from His word? How does He see me according to His word? This was a critical and necessary step if I was going to remove the muzzle. I learned that my relationship with God's word was imperative and that building my self-esteem was just as important as drinking water and eating food each day. If I missed building myself in the word of God, I would feel sluggish, fatigued and even exhausted.

4. **Use my cup as a weapon.** After filling my cup, I now have a weapon that must be used. Instead of allowing negative thoughts to invade my space, I choose to use the promises of God from my cup as a weapon. Challenges will come. So many times, I forgot my cup was full of weapons. Either I could sit in defeat or get up and use my weapons against this muzzle sent to destroy me. I needed to use my weapons to remove me from the toxic relationship that I welcomed because I did not set proper boundaries. The removal of the muzzle allowed me to see where I needed to use my weapons. Sitting in toxic relationships was not God's best for my life. If people did not welcome my authenticity, it was a toxic relationship. If I had to be something other than my authentic self, it was a toxic relationship. This is my personal definition of a toxic relationship. A toxic relationship is any relationship where your authenticity is not welcomed or stifled, any relationship where you are encouraged to morph into something that you were not created to become. Identify toxic relationships and use your weapons from your cup to remove yourself from the

toxic environment. If you choose to stay, you are welcoming a muzzle.

5. **<u>Train people how to treat you</u>**. This begins first with treating yourself with respect on every level and setting boundaries. Now you are ready to share these boundaries with others. People will treat you the way that you allow them to treat you. The muzzle allowed the real me not to speak up for myself. Once this muzzle was removed my voice emerged and I had to establish new boundaries for my life. When I set boundaries, every relationship that did not want to adhere to my new standards fell off. It was painful to lose a few people, but it was necessary. It was either me or them and for years—yes, years—it had been about everyone else, to my detriment. I needed to show people how to treat me. I needed to let them know what was acceptable and what was not acceptable. I needed to be happy with shedding relationships that did not celebrate my freedom but instead embraced the muzzled me. I was no longer muzzled so I could no longer allow myself to be treated the way I allowed when I was muzzled. It was liberating. It was exciting. There was so much freedom in my voice. There is so much peace in my soul. My relationships are authentic because I am authentic with myself.

My Day of Liberation

One day after ministering in service, as I was leaving the platform a man stopped me and said, "I love it when you preach and give declarations. You have such a roar. There is a sound in your voice that touches heaven and shakes the atmosphere. Your voice has tremendous power. Your sound is mighty." I replied, "Thank you so much. You have no idea how powerful your words are to me." I quickly exited the building to get to my car because I could feel my emotions bubbling up. Once inside my car, door closed and locked, the tears began to fall down my cheeks. My eyes closed and my hands lifted in worship. I knew that the fight and struggle was not about me, but it was about what God created me to be. It was about my purpose and what I was destined to complete. I sat for a few more minutes in worship, smiling, laughing, and just thanking God for being with me on this journey as He has always been in my life. I replayed that conversation again in my head... "Your voice has tremendous power. Your sound is mighty." I whispered to myself, "Your sound is mighty."

In that moment everything made sense and the muzzle had absolutely no victory in my life. I knew that my part of my purpose was to free other women from their muzzles and allow their true selves to emerge and live. In that moment it made sense to me. My voice, my physical voice, was a weapon. My voice was free! I was free to be me! I was free to love me! I was free to see myself through the loving eyes of God! I was FREE!

There is nothing like being and loving yourself, without pretense or judgment or trying to fit in with others. I am beyond happy to get my voice back and be who God created me to be...uniquely ME!!

Prayer of Encouragement

Father, I place every painful word that has been spoken over my life in your hands. I give the words and the pain completely to you. I ask for your healing power to cover my heart and my emotions that were damaged through these painful words. I thank you that the blood of your son Jesus has the power to heal my damaged emotions and remove the sting of the painful memories from my heart and mind. I choose freedom on this day and to walk in authenticity with myself first, then others. I choose to see myself the way that you view me, and that is healed and whole, nothing missing, and nothing broken. Your word is a shield around my heart. Thank you for loving me and caring for me. You are indeed a Good Father and I thank you for my voice! Thank you for my voice!

Now every daughter who believes she is welcome to sit in a space of freedom and grace, unmuzzled and without shame, stand up today in your freedom.

Let your authentic VOICE ARISE!

Karen serves as a catalyst for transformation, growth and development. She is passionate about collaborating and working in partnerships with others. As individuals and organizations journey to new or higher heights and horizons, Karen serves as a champion each step of the way.

Karen holds a Master's degree in Social Work and serves as a Life Coach while supporting individuals, leaders, and workforce development. Karen is CEO and Founder of KDT Global Consulting which focuses to serve individuals, families and couples as they evolve and grow. Also, with zeal, Karen partners with, assists and equips leaders and organizations through the process of growth and development while creating and implementing strategic plans.

Karen adores her husband, parents, siblings, and enjoys her exciting journey of her blended family of ten (four adult children, two teenagers, one daughter-in-law and three grandchildren).

Karen serves as a torch that ignites and shines possibilities to others.

I DO HAVE A VOICE

Karen Tyler

Walk with me as I share my journey of freedom as I boldly and courageously discover and embrace that "I do have a voice." Experience my journey with me as I walk in the liberty of being set free from other people, limitations and being placed in boxes. This is only the beginning of my journey. I welcome you to boldly and courageously begin to step out of boxes as you discover that you have choices and a voice to be heard. Embrace it.

As I sat staring at the bright sky while the sun beamed on my face, there were so many feelings emerging. Feelings of excitement, relief and joy, as well as feelings of anxiety and discomfort as I realized, "I do have a voice." "I do have a choice." "I am not crazy." I am a person who has thoughts, opinions, options and a voice to be heard. For years and years and years, my voice has been silenced, little by little. For far too long, my choices have been altered, and my mouth muzzled as I've been placed in a box with a pretty bow. Such boxes have shaped, formed and cultivated my daily existence, my choices, and my decisions. All were held tightly by the boxes that I tried to fit in and stay in but found myself busting the lid off and bursting out of the box as a reaction and not because I was responding. It was out of frustration, anger, or just being tired of being held hostage. The box was tight, limiting, constricting and heavy because I've always known there was something more outside the box, something more to life.

"Karen, be quiet," they said. "Karen, you can't say that; you can't do that," they said. "Karen, do the right thing, say the right thing." "Karen, just leave it alone." "Don't you go stirring up stuff." I vividly remember the looks, the stares and the unspoken gestures that presented a clear understanding that I better not move or say a word. I am the "why" chick, who really only wants to understand, especially when things don't add up or make sense or aren't clear. I am the logical one who asks questions (well, at least tries to) as I observe, process and draw conclusions.

Sometimes as I speak, the words come out of my mouth and internally, my voice sounds low and muffled. Sometimes I just sit with a lump in my throat. Other times I feel heavy after being shut down and set down. Am I not important? Do I not matter? Does what I have to say mean anything? Then I began to become comfortable with it, because you know, "That's just the way it is." "It is what it is." And who wants to continue to fight all the time? Who wants to continue to be shut down? It's just physically, emotionally and mentally exhausting. So I did the next best thing. I learned how to fly under the radar. I earned an Emmy Award for "being in the back" and an Oscar award for "just sucking it up."

Until one day, my moment of examining being in a box arrived. As I sat in a class, the leader stated, "I need a volunteer for a demonstration." As I paused and waited before I responded (because you know, I've learned the behavior to just be and sit quietly), my hand slowly slid up as I said, "I'll do it." Just the way the leader said, "Great," and smiled, I thought, *Oh my, here I go.* And then she began sharing the following: "Thank you for volunteering; feel free to discontinue participating at any time," and that's when I took a DEEP breath. Then I thought, *Oh my goodness Karen, what are you doing?* But I was curious as I always am, and this was just to volunteer for a demonstration, so why couldn't it be me?

The transformation of my life began, and everything was going well, until she began asking me about my experience and my feelings. Immediately, my face turned stone cold, my heart began to race and it felt like a tractor was lying on my chest. The discussion turned into us having a conversation about me being a perfectionist and being controlling. We talked about how I grew too rigid and my having a LOW tolerance for foolishness. Then we were off to a conversation about my impatience with people asking for forgiveness when they should have asked for permission up front. My impatience with people using omission, not telling the truth, being real or keeping their word, led to me talking about the impact of being let down, hurt and disappointed. We began to talk about the walls I have put up in my life—walls that are constructed to protect me, physically, emotionally and mentally.

As we talked, I began to connect with the boxes that others had placed me in. I also peeked inside boxes I created and placed my own self in. And then she asked me to curl myself up as if I was in a box. I thought, *That's it; this woman is crazy*, but I had already gone too far and an inner part of me wanted to continue. I wanted to continue to understand and have insight. As I rolled up tightly, with my head tucked tightly into my arms as my face was buried in my lap, I experienced the feeling of being squished in a box. As we continued to talk the tears began to flow. I had an out-of-body experience as I began to become even more transparent as I faced a few realities I had turned a blind eye to while my voice was silenced down through the years. Although I was struggling with the experience of being still rolled up as if I was in a box, I began to understand some things as I listened to my own voice. There were no barriers this time, no one telling me "Don't say that," "no," "stop," "don't do that," "don't think that." For once in my life (FINALLY) I was given permission to be me, to be real, honest, to remove the covering from my mouth, as I connected with "my voice," as I connected "with me," with my truth and reality, for the very first time.

I cried a lot as snot drained from my nose. I cried some more, and my nose drained even more. As I unfolded myself and looked up, I was a mess. And oh, did I mention this was in front of a classroom full of people? The room was so quiet you could hear a pin drop on cotton. During the demonstration, I had disconnected from everything and everybody, to the point that nothing mattered but me breaking free—breaking free from boxes, bondage, other people, group thinking and "the way it's supposed to be" (well, according to who and what?). The experience was about ten minutes, and it felt like forever. I began to put myself back together again as I fixed my shirt (it was so disheveled) and had to catch my breath. The tears continued to roll down my face like Niagara Falls and tissue stuck to my face like gum on the sidewalk. Gee, I was trying to be cool and reserved, and at the same time, I didn't care. The feeling of freedom was awesome while that silencing voice tried to continue to stop me from experiencing the process.

But may I say how liberating (and embarrassing) the opportunity was to experience someone give me permission to speak my truth and for my peers to create a safe environment that was accepting and non-judgmental, and they held the space for me. The thrilling feeling I experienced, despite the feelings of shame, guilt, anger and disappointment, is indescribable, as was the release, the freedom, the breakthrough and deliverance that I experienced as I had the courage and boldness to speak my truth. I learned that things are not about me being controlling; it's about me having control, not being controlled. It's about me being released from the expectations of people, rules and rituals, etc. It's about me bursting through barriers of roles of women, historical race and cultural limitations and pieces of historical family practices that were not befitting. It's about me not being bound to religion or legalism and instead, being free to be in relationship with God, adhering to sound doctrine and not man-imposed guidelines.

So what has opened up for me? Permission to be me, to be honest, transparent, and authentic as I realize and embrace "I do have a voice." I began to connect with the concept that it's okay to allow myself to be vulnerable (how frightening), to have own my emotions, to express my emotions and to embrace that I do not have to be strong all the time. I can use my voice to share how I really feel. I accept that I don't have to be perfect and it's okay to allow myself space to make mistakes. And the beauty of all of this is that I still have value; I am still worthy and qualified. I began to feel like a little girl on Christmas morning, running from gift to gift, from box to box. And guess what? Gifts belong in boxes, not voices, not me, not you, not people. I can make choices based on my voice and then share my choice as I stand in my truth and no longer live in boxes.

After I eventually got myself together (it felt like it was a LONG time), I made it through the class for the day and just sat while reflecting. I smiled, and tears began to roll down my face again as I confirmed for myself, *I have a voice. I have a choice.* As I reflected, I decided I would no longer live in the historical box of limitations. I would no longer be quieted by race and culture. You know, the one that says, "Shh, don't speak, don't think, just do as you're told." Or "you're black and therefore you can't," or "that's not for you."

I recall an incident as a young girl. My friends were preparing to go to the mall. We had guests over at that time who questioned if we should be allowed to go because, "You know we shouldn't go past the main street into the white neighborhood." There it was: a deposit into my spirit and a push into a box. "Well, why can't I?" And "who said so?" Now I know I can use my voice to speak when I disagree.

I recall when I was preparing to attend college. A well-known person who supported youth with obtaining scholarship money told me as I asked about the college I attended, "You can't go there; you won't make it." He began to share statistics of how many blacks weren't successful in graduating from this school and how it takes five to six years for blacks to complete a four-year program. "This is according to who, and why is this?" Well, I used my voice as I exercised my choice (I didn't realize it back then), went to that college anyway and graduated in four years with my Bachelor's degree. After attending for a total of five years, I graduated again, earning my Master's degree. I did that even in the face of sitting in one of my first college courses and experiencing overt racism. My learned behavior of being silent kept my mouth shut, until one day, he did it again. I kicked the top off the box and used my voice that had been muzzled. *This is enough.* I was paying tuition just like everyone else and I deserved to be there just like everyone else. I opened my mouth and nicely, yet in a firm way, let him know his behavior was unacceptable. The room was so quiet you could hear a pin drop in sugar. No one in the room parted their lips besides me and no one moved as I sat in my chair. As I used my voice, as

I glanced around the room and stared everyone directly in their eyes, I began to feel liberated. I even addressed my professor, still in a nice, firm, respectful way, and she was clear that racism was no longer acceptable. "I do have a voice."

As I further reflected, I decided I would no longer live in the box of roles for women or be quieted. You know, the box that says, "Shh, don't speak, don't think, just follow instructions." You know, the box of roles that says, "You can only cook, clean, have babies and be domesticated." Now there is nothing wrong with any of these things; I do them all. What I'm referring to is this expectation that has been presumed from women. I will no longer live in the box or roles that have designated jobs as those of librarians, care providers and teachers, just to name a few. I have a choice. I have a voice. My voice matters as I share what works for me, and that I don't have to live up to society's expectations.

Ahhh, how refreshing to know and understand I have a voice! How releasing it is to embrace my truth and live, opposed to being bound by race, culture and roles. Then there's the suffocation box of religion and legalism. I yearned to be free, to have a pure relationship with God, and not be measured by man's-imposed guidelines, but couldn't speak it. I was hindered by the box that says, "You can't wear red lipstick or red pantyhose." The box of "music and dancing are bad" when in fact music and dancing was part of the biblical process for many purposes. The crazy didn't stop; then it was, "Women cannot hold certain roles," and the box was crystal clear, as women weren't permitted to speak while standing in the same spot as men. "What was really happening?" "Do not ask questions and listen to what I say," they said. Where does any of this hold true and what bearing does it have on salvation?

I recall being "provided permission" by leaders to wear pants. However, when I went to a venue for a course, I was greatly chastised by another leader while being told wearing pants wasn't acceptable. After completing the course, there was a main event and directives were given to remove all earrings. While attempting to seek clarity and insight as to how this aligned with the doctrine that was just taught, of course, the limitation and silencing box appeared. As I began to ask questions, of course, I was silenced and told, "When in Rome, do as the Romans do." I respect the expectations of any house. My confusion emerges as these expectations are flushed with bad doctrine followed by compliance. Contrary to popular belief, it's okay to speak, ask questions and make inquiries about things you don't understand.

I am excited for my freedom road to empowerment. I am thankful that I raised my hand, did a simple thing as I used my voice to utter two words, "I'll volunteer." Wow, my journey is just beginning and I have a lot of work to do as I begin to voice my needs, set boundaries and share them with others while crawling out of boxes. The learned behaviors of not speaking while "following protocol" must be unlearned. It takes time and I will stand in what's important to me—freedom, peace and purpose—as I use my voice to speak.

Take a DEEP breath. You, too, have permission to use your voice. Use it; give yourself permission to speak while seeking clarity and asking questions. What are your boxes? What structures exist that have been created for you? Keep in mind, some boxes and structures are out of our control and others exist that you may find more difficult to get out of. Even then, your voice is important and needed to share your boundaries that will provide you more space and freedom, right in the box where you sit. Having crucial conversations while sharing our thoughts, opinions and beliefs is okay. Otherwise, silence and confinement will eat us alive, or we'll continue coming out of the box swinging because of anger, hurt, fear, frustration and reacting as our voice is shared.

Take a DEEP breath as you pause, assess situations, look at things from all perspectives. Then determine your yeses and your noes, as well as what you are willing to live with and what you can't live with. Examine all the possibilities and outcomes while you make a choice, not based on the boxes, limitations or structures but a choice based on a sound decision you have made. And then use your voice to share your thoughts, opinions and boundaries as you share your needs and make your requests. In the end, write your own story. Although your story has begun to be written for you, you take the pen and begin to complete your own story. As you do, you'll untie your mouth while using your voice to walk boldly and courageously in freedom and peace. "You do have a voice—use it!!"

Tanya Chenese Young, educator, mentor, and spiritual leader, loves serving the families of her Decatur, Illinois community. She desires to assist those traumatized from loss to healing. She is the co-founder (with late husband Larry D. Young) of Way of Life Christian Center. Her greatest challenge was taking the helm as interim pastor, after her husband's sudden, unexpected transition to eternity.

Tanya's passion for education reflects in the success of those she has served for 32 years as teacher, facilitator, coach, assistant principal and principal. Recently retired, Tanya volunteers as an empowerment leader for Sherrod's Independent. Mentoring Program (SIMP) Inc.

She is currently pursuing her Doctor of Ministry in Biblical Counseling.

Tanya's affirmation: I lead, I serve, and I empower! "I can do all things through Christ who strengthens me"! (Philippians 4:13, NKJV)

JOY RESTORED

Tanya Young

> Exodus 15:20, NLT
> *Then Miriam the prophet, Aaron's sister,*
> *took a tambourine and led all the women as*
> *they played their tambourines and danced.*

I rise early in the morning and say, "Thank you, God!" As my feet hit the floor I proclaim, "Today is a good day to be a good day." Readiness for the day includes prayer, praise and meditation. I also include mindful/gratitude moments, forgiveness and words of affirmation.

Getting my mom ready for the day is an added blessing. As I prepare her breakfast, I command Alexa to play my playlist. From Mary Mary's "I'm Walking" to Bill Withers' "Lovely Day," the small space in my kitchen becomes my dance floor. While flipping pancakes or scrambling eggs I dance, sing and laugh at an occasional glimpse of myself in the window, and repeat, "Thank you, God! Today is a good day to be a good day!"

These are my intentional mornings today. Dance enhances my posture of gratitude and allows me to grab my happiness. It breathes in life and exhales light. I embrace the music and step to the beat of my favorite songs, commanding joy, instead of and sometimes in spite of circumstances.

However, on the morning of August 21, 2013, instead of rising and saying, "Thank you, God," I was awakened by what seemed to be a cry for help. I jumped up and ran down the stairs to my mom's room. She was fast asleep. It was my husband. I ran back upstairs and opened the door, where I found him. With shallow breaths, he was unable to speak. I ran for my phone to call 911. The dispatcher instructed me to get him to the floor and guided me through the initial steps of CPR as he took his last breath. I frantically grabbed him and said, "You can't go!" The para-medics arrived at that moment. I watched as if it were a movie. It was almost like I was disconnected from the scene. I recall asking multiple times if he was breathing and the answer was, "No ma'am, he is not." It seemed like they worked on him for hours. Still unable to resuscitate, they made the decision to take him to the nearest hospital. It was there that he was pronounced deceased from a massive heart attack. The coroner described it as an internal explosion and said he was certain that my husband felt no pain.

On this morning heaven gained a warrior and I lost my best friend, lover, confidant, covering and partner in life. On this morning I was knocked off of my feet. This is the day the music stopped playing, or maybe I stopped hearing it. On this day my world, as I grew to love and cherish it, came crashing down. It felt as if the rug had been pulled from under me. The love of my life was gone! I couldn't find the rhythm or even reach for a song. It was so unex-pected, and such an intimate departure.

My husband had been diagnosed with Polymyositis (pol-e-my-o-SY-tis), an uncommon inflammatory disease that causes muscle weakness affecting both sides of the body. Having this condition can make it difficult to climb stairs, rise from a seated position, lift objects or reach overhead. It could be extremely painful, but he never complained. He was undergoing an aggressive form of treatment which resulted in intermittent improvement, but also measurable decline. After his first year of treatment, we decided to seek a second opinion. We drove to a neighboring state to see a specialist. It was a beautiful day. We met with the specialist. She confirmed that his treatment was appropriate and, although it was aggressive, the road to recovery might take some time. The only additional recommendation was for him to have an EKG. She would forward her recommendation to his specialist back home. We left her office feeling very encouraged.

We made an impromptu lunch date and stopped at one of the area's popular and famous restaurants. My husband was not impressed at all! We laughed as he joked about the hype. After lunch, we stopped for ice cream cones and competed to see who would lose by eating theirs first. Great conversations, lots of laughter—it was such a beautiful day in so many ways. We arrived home that evening, checked in on Mom and shared the good news that we received from the specialist. It was a little late for dinner, so we opted for fruit bowls. After he sliced the watermelon, he took my hand and we began to dance, just a little two-step. I recall thinking, *What song could be playing in his head?*—our inside joke. I often teased him that his favorite songs were before my time. What a great way to end a great day. I did not know that this would be our last day to laugh together, dance together, spend the night together.

James 4:14, NIV

Why, you do not even know what will happen tomorrow.
What is your life? You are a mist that appears
for a little while and then vanishes.

The impact of the early morning events on August 21, 2013 was overwhelming. I had experienced loss before, but nothing seemed to compare to the depth of pain that I was experiencing. I wanted to understand. I couldn't control my response. I tried to find my rhythm but didn't recognize the song. I was going through the motions, trying to embrace the support of family and friends, orchestrating the celebration of life of this amazing husband, father, grandfather, community leader, pastor and teacher, trudging through the pain. I was literally pushing it down, while covered with emptiness and loneliness, trying to do my best to encourage those who were integral parts of the familiar song with him, now behind us.

I had so many questions. One time I actually yelled out, "God, why? Help me understand!" I wondered; *Did I miss something? Could I have done something? What if I had gotten to him sooner— would he still be here? Should we have sought a second opinion earlier?* Questions upon questions, ongoing conversations with God. This was so heavy.

I researched his condition. I wanted to know what others living with polymyositis were experiencing. Were there any documented deaths similar to his? I found that there are estimated to be somewhere between one and eight cases per million people—such a rare and unusual condition. The overall mortality rate is 1.75 to 2.92, with women experiencing death more than men. There was only one similar death documented, a young woman in the UK. The condition was uncovered during an autopsy, after she passed.

My whys became louder; the grief couldn't be any heavier. I returned to work and accepted the position of interim pastor of the church that my husband and I had launched only three years prior to his transition. I gradually busied myself in the positions of caregiver, principal and pastor. Trying to balance this amidst overwhelming grief and unanswered questions seemed impossible most days. But it was the moments outside of school and church that were clear reminders that I was barely standing.

Weeping may endure for a night, but joy comes in the morning. Grief is deep sorrow, especially that caused by someone's death. Where was my morning? I sought God continuously. I needed to understand my grief, my response to this loss. I felt that I couldn't effectively support others who were struggling with similar loss.

I've always faced life's challenges—and there have been many!—through the eyes of faith. But somewhere in my early Christian development, I learned the practice of showing up strong, almost as if your strength measured your faith—as if it wasn't ok NOT to be ok. In my past experiences, questioning God was minimum. I learned to push my grief down and suffer in silence. I learned to show up ok, even when I was not ok. But this time was different. I was screaming, *Lord, why?* I wanted to also understand my overwhelming grief.

Proverbs 4:7, KJV
Wisdom is the principal thing; therefore, get wisdom:
and with all thy getting get understanding.

One particular day, at a principals' meeting, a colleague approached me and asked, "How are you doing?" I was asked that question a lot and most of the time I'd reply that I was ok. But this time I answered, "At the moment OK, but most days I don't really know how I'm doing." His response was, "I know where you are. I've been there." He began to share his story. He lost his wife during childbirth. They were young, fresh out of college, on their own and away from family. He was alone, with his first child, an infant, and beginning life as a new father and as a widower. There were similarities: My baby was the toddler ministry, just three years old; I was far away from my biological family, but thanking God for my bonus children, sister in love, nieces and church family. He shared that he was the facilitator of a grief workshop at his church and encouraged me to come. The timing could not have been more perfect. A new class was about to begin. I had a moment as I conversed with him, recalling a conversation with a dear friend who checked in with me every day. She would ask, "Tanya, are you ok?" And I would say "I'm ok." She always knew what my reality was and she would respond, "You're not ok." She suggested that I seek help or talk to someone.

I registered with the church then began my personal research on grief. I used the excuse that I wanted to front load information in preparation for the workshop. Hearing someone else's story elevated me in some kind of way. I read every article that I could find. I ordered a few books and engaged with online resources, while continuing to take my daily dose of God's word, posting power scriptures in my office (home and school), on my bathroom mirror, in my car:

Psalm 34:18, ESV
The Lord is near to the brokenhearted and saves the crushed in spirit.

2 Corinthians 1:3-4, ESV
Blessed be the God and Father of our Lord Jesus Christ, the Father of mercies and God of all comfort, who comforts us in all our affliction, so that we may be able to comfort those who are in any affliction, with the comfort with which we ourselves are comforted by God.

Psalms 147:3, NIV
He heals the brokenhearted and binds up their wounds.

Just a few.

I learned that there were two models of the stages of grief and loss. The first model indicated that there were five stages: denial, anger, bargaining, depression, and acceptance. The second model indicated seven stages: shock, denial, depression, anger, testing, decision, and integration. As I unpacked the characteristics of these stages, I began to understand grief.

Shock: intense and sometimes paralyzing surprise at the loss.

Denial: disbelief and the need to look for evidence to confirm the loss.

Anger and frustration: a mix between acknowledgment that some things have changed and anger at this change.

Depression: lack of energy and intense sadness.

Testing: experimenting with the new situation to discover what it actually means in your life.

Decision: a rising optimism about learning how to manage the new situation.

Integration: acceptance of the new reality, reflection on what you learned, and stepping out in the world as a renewed person.

Bargaining is the melody to the steady beat of guilt. This is when you endure the endless "what if" statements.

Treatment is an added stage that may be applied when someone is experiencing long-term depression, anxiety or temporary symptoms of physical illness resulting from grief. For example, when someone experiences a shocking event, the body releases stress hormones. These hormones can cause part of the heart to briefly swell and stop pumping. The remaining parts continue beating as normal, causing an uneven flow of blood. A person may experience intense chest pain, mimicking a heart attack (but the arteries are not blocked like a heart attack). This malfunction, a temporary state, is called "broken heart syndrome."

Proverbs 4:7, KJV
Wisdom is the principal thing; therefore, get wisdom: and with all thy getting get understanding.

The lyrics to the song that was playing in my soul became clearer. I acquired the language that I needed to pray, to apply prescribed scripture, to communicate with others, and to be able to process my personal journey and my road to healing. Every one handles grief in their own way. I wanted to be transparent. Yes, I am a woman of faith and my Lord and Savior and I are tight. But there were many days when I was not ok. And it was definitely ok, not to be ok. To fake it, like many of us do, is dishonest and denies the power of God to work in us and through us.

Looking forward to the grief workshop, I still had so many questions and some "how-tos" to uncover. I was so ready to receive this intervention. I wanted to be restored. You see, I was pouring out, without a refilling. I was putting the oxygen mask on others without having one for myself. What a revelation!

I joined a community of widows and widowers at the workshop. We were able to share our stories, support one another, and gain more insight from our facilitator. I gained more knowledge, understanding and strategies from a facilitator who had walked in our shoes. I was able to connect with women and men who were grieving. I had the language to share my journey. It was a blessing to give and to receive from this group of amazing people. We were all striving to heal, striving to understand, striving to transition to a solo dance and recapture the joys of new life.

Proverbs 27:17, NIV
As iron sharpens iron, so one person sharpens another.

Connecting to community was the pivotal point of my journey. I learned that a common community has great potential to support healing. I also learned the positive attributes of grief. I began to slowly choreograph the steps in integrating this new knowledge into my life.

I connected to other communities: a grief support group that was facilitated by the chaplain at the hospital, a pastoral alliance partnership covered me and increased my knowledge and skills in faith based organizational leadership, and a female clergy support group provided a safe place of continued healing and restoration.

Philippians 4:13, NLT
I can do all this through him who gives me strength.

The lyrics and the melody of my grief were unlocked and a new song of transition was unfolding. Gradually and slowly, my steps increased and my new dance took shape and form. I was able to step into my healing with an understanding that when sudden, traumatic grief causes you to cycle through the stages of denial, anger, bargaining, depression and acceptance, you are also protected by these stages as you attempt to process change and adapt to your new reality.

I learned to step into self-awareness, self-forgiveness, and self-care. I two-stepped my way into transparency and openness, accepting help and asking for help, when needed. I pivoted, intentionally, toward things that made me happy.

Was this transition easy? Absolutely not! Did grief go away? I don't believe it will ever go away for me but it does NOT remain the same. Time and technique help to manage it. The hope lies in knowing that God is a healer. There's confidence in Him to renew, restore and rebuild the empty spaces of our hearts.

Traumatic grief may manifest in a variety of ways. DON'T BE AFRAID TO ASK FOR HELP.

After a while, maybe close to a year, I began to experience sleep deprivation.

But it was unlike the lack of sleep at the beginning of my grief journey. I would actually fall asleep quite easily and then abruptly wake up. It felt like a panic attack. After some weeks of experiencing this, I made an appointment to talk with my physician. He was my husband's physician as well, so I felt comfortable seeking his advice. We had a long conversation about diet, exercise and what prompted my visit: lack of sleep. He suggested that I see a grief counselor. I was still in the space where my husband transitioned. Yes, I redecorated, moved some things around, got rid of some old things and introduced new items to the space, but it was still in the space where he transitioned.

I took his advice and made an appointment with a Christian counselor. Through a therapeutic process the counselor determined that I was suffering from a mild case of post-traumatic stress disorder. The sudden impact of losing him, the fact that he died not just in my presence but literally in my arms, could've had a lasting impact or effect on me psychologically. We scheduled a series of sessions and I learned to incorporate emotional freedom technique (EFT). EFT is an alternative treatment for physical pain and emotional distress. It's also referred to as tapping or psychological acupressure. Tapping the body in acupressure points can create a balance in your energy system and treat pain. This technique is highly effective with children and adults who struggle socially and emotionally, and who have experienced trauma. Well, it worked! I still use EFT today to minimize stress and anxiety. We are social, emotional, physical, psychological, and spiritual beings, complex individuals. God makes provisions on the earth to minister to all of our complexities.

I reached that pivotal moment in my journey where I understood my song. The choreography, the routine, and even additional dancers became a part of my new song. I could now reflect on the tears I cried, prayers I prayed, help I sought, my community connections, the help God sent, and the healing that he so divinely orchestrated. I could now reflect on the past memories of my life with my amazing husband, with tears sometimes, coupled with experiencing the joy. I express my gratitude for the special time we had together. My self-awareness and self-care allowed me to enjoy my children and my grandchildren, my family and my friends immensely. Sharing my story gave me an avenue to help others who are experiencing loss in so many ways. I found my way back to living and really enjoying the things that make me happy. Traveling, the arts, especially theater, a great film, the beach, Maryland seafood (overnight shipping), float therapy, European facials, and of course, music and dancing.

I rise early in the morning and say, "Thank you God!" As my feet hit the floor I proclaim, "Today is a good day to be a good day." Readiness for the day includes prayer, praise and meditation. I also include mindful/gratitude moments, forgiveness and words of affirmation.

I intentionally reach for my happiness with expectation. Joy restored!

Dr. J. Michelle Vann serves the community as an author, educator, life coach, and motivational speaker. She is an Amazon bestselling author that loves to help women heal, mind, body, and spirit.

Michelle is the owner of Vanntastic Solutions a wellness coach practice and the founder of Sistahs Can We Talk, a nonprofit helping women fill the gap in their disparities of health.

She lives by this quote from George Benard Shaw *"I am of the opinion that my life belongs to the community, and as long as I live, it is my privilege to do for it whatever I can. I want to be thoroughly used up when I die, for the harder I work, the more I live. Life is no 'brief candle' to me. It is a sort of splendid torch which I have got hold of for a moment..."*

FILLING THE DAD-SIZED HOLE

Dr. J. Michelle Vann

I do not think that I had ever seen my husband as happy as he was when we gave birth to our first child. Do not get me wrong; he was thrilled the second time, but he was more prepared. He said over and over, "I don't know if I can hold a baby." Fortunately for him, our baby was nine pounds and 21 inches long, so he was not so little. I watched him oh-so-gently slip his hands under our newborn child's head and back and bring him to his broad chest as he held on for dear life. These were the days before skin-to-skin contact was a thing. Our baby knew his dad was a little scared because he just snuggled in like, "Let me help you, Dad." My husband wanted to connect with his son. With that same love and care, two years later, we had a beautiful little girl—so perfect and a little smaller (fortunately for me). He was ready this time, prepared to scoop her up and pretend that she was a football just like he had practiced over the last few years. He had this now. His little princess was safe in his arms.

That safety seemed to shatter overnight when I noticed our baby was yellow. While the nurse tried to argue that I did not know what I was talking about, I knew. So I put her in the window to let the sun shine on her, hoping that would be enough to get her system in gear. Unfortunately, it was not. She would have to be placed in the Neonatal Intensive Care Unit. She looked like she was on the mother ship. Every light that could be around her was, and it was scary. After five days, I was dismissed, and she was not. I remember the concern in my husband's eyes that we would be leaving our daughter there. Her case was much more severe than her brother's. We stayed at the hospital until they kicked us out for the night. Oh, I could see the concern in his big brown eyes as he stared at his baby girl with all of those lights. The only thing we could do was pray. Each day when we went to be with her, he cradled her and sang to her as only a daddy could. When it got a little dicey and they talked about blood transfusions, I saw him step to his Father. He began to pray for our sweet little baby as he caressed her back ever so gently. Wow, the love of a father.

As I think back to that, I could get a little jealous. Please, do not get me wrong. My husband makes me feel special, but he is not my father. It has been said that a father holds his daughter's hand for a short while, but he holds her heart forever. That is a feeling that I will never know. While I made sure that my children had their father in their life, that was not the case for me.

I was born into a prominent religious family within our small community—spiritual enough to say that having a baby out of wedlock was wrong, but not too holy to offer an alternative. My mother had an option, yet she chose to bring me into this world. This is very likely the place in which rejection was placed in my heart. That same rejection created a dad-sized hole in my heart. I have never known the caress of the man whose DNA pulses through my veins.

Back to this big crazy family that I would not trade for the world: My mom, like many other moms, worked to make ends meet. My auntie-mom decided that I should live with them. My mom could get me any time she wanted, but it would give me stability to live with Auntie-mom. Before we go further, I do not want you, ever, to get the wrong idea. Like many single moms in America, my mom is great, and she did what was needed to survive. It is easy to judge until you walk in someone's shoes; you really cannot appreciate their struggle. So I do not share to tear down, but to encourage every single mom to keep pushing.

Living with my great uncle, auntie-mom, and cousin-sister was incredible. I was the only kid, and I was often loved so much that I forgot that my dad was not present. My uncles, grandfather, and godfather made sure that I had everything that I wanted. One might say that I was a little spoiled. Maybe? Anyway, it didn't dawn on me that my dad was absent until there were events at school that required a dad. Fortunately, back then, those were few and far between, but they existed. My godfather would show up and hang out for a few of us. I wasn't the only kid from a single-parent family.

One day, I can remember being in a department store, and there was this lady who kept following me around the store. At first, I didn't think too much about it. I am from a tiny, very white town, so having someone follow the black kid in the store was not strange, just irritating. However, this was different. She was watching me and, at this point, making me feel a bit uncomfortable. What did this crazy lady want? I was about to go and ask when my mother grabbed my shoulder and said, "Let us go." What? Who was that? She said she would explain in the car. Well, that was my bio dad's mother. Um, why couldn't she just come over and say something and not be weird? I was in middle school at this time and was turned off by this crazy behavior. It was then that I decided that I wanted nothing to do with any of them and that they had missed out on a fabulous treat. I was the bomb. That is why she couldn't help but stare.

But that dad-sized hole would pop up in other strange ways. I wanted the attention of older boys, and because I was pretty cute with really long, silky hair, I got any boy that I wanted. Now, the fact that I wasn't putting out caused a problem, but I could get 'em. As I went into high school, I had never processed my great-grandmother's death when I was ten, and the depression cycle that I found myself in was all-consuming. I only wore black and white the whole school year, I barely ate, and I cried in private every day. I learned to fake the funk. I was dying on the inside, but I learned to put on the mask so that nobody really knew what was happening. Every now and then, someone would push the right button, and it would reveal my hole. Looking back, I don't know how I graduated.

Interestingly enough, while I had so many people around me, nobody knew what was going on in my life. I never had that person who made me follow through with anything. I was on the volleyball team, but I quit the day before the first game because I didn't think I was good enough. I took the most uncomplicated math because nobody was tuned in to push me. I always wondered if my dad had been present, if things would have been different.

I also think that missing out on my dad's time pushed me to marry much earlier than I should have. Don't get me wrong, I have a fabulous husband and would not change anything about our marriage. I just think that I would not have been looking so early.

I read a book by Dr. David G. Evans where he talks about all of the scars that people have from various traumas in their lives, and he shared an idea that transformed how I looked at my life. Every little girl has in her mind this picture of a knight in shining armor who will sweep her off her feet and take her off to a fairy tale life. He explains that this ideology only leads to disappointment for all involved because, in this situation, somebody's expectations will not be met. When I understood this, I finally realized that I had secretly been sabotaging my relationship, expecting my husband to fill that knight in shining armor's shoes, not a husband's space. I can remember during this time I would remind him that he wasn't my dad. This was not his problem; it was mine, but all tied to my hole that I was trying to fill.

I kept telling myself that I didn't need a dad. I was fine, but my kids would ask why they didn't have two grandpas like other kids. So I spoke with my mom, and we decided to go and talk with him. At this point, I did not need a dad, I needed closure.

We drove to my hometown, and upon arrival, we stopped at my grandmother's house. She was a beautiful soul we were slowly losing to dementia, but she was still able to live in her house. We spent some time with her and had a few other errands to run. While out, she called and said that she had lost her wallet and was very upset. If you knew my grandma, she always had a wad of cash, so we had to find this wallet. We found it on the couch. Grandma, why? This little venture did not leave us anytime to see the bio-dude. Bummer!

As we headed back over the highway, we discussed the next time we would approach him. He was in the hospital when we were there, and we would not have found him at home. I never had any ill-will for him. I just wanted him to do what was right. Again, I did not want anything from him, just closure. To my dismay, I got a call the very next day saying that he had a heart attack overnight and had passed away. What? Really? I just got the nerve to approach this buster, and now he is dead? Come on, God.

I decided that I would attend the funeral to see if I could see people, characteristics, and other signs that I fit in. We went from the funeral home to the cemetery, and everything within me wanted to scream. I wanted to ask if they saw me. Did they know me? However, my bigger self said that this event was not about me. Those kids who were sitting on the front row did not know me, and their daddy had just died. He was never coming back for them, and they had a relationship. I did not. Everything in me wanted to walk up to that casket, grab his lifeless body and shake him like a rag doll to ask him why, but he was dead.

Death was final, and I still didn't have any answers. There was a cousin who figured it out right away and engaged with me. She asked me what my story was. Who was I? She started talking to me about this family that I was watching. Wow, someone had seen me. While everyone else just stared at me, she saw me. I was looking, and they were looking. It was the most awkward repast dinner I have ever attended, and trust me, I have seen some crazy things happen at funeral repast dinners. I kept telling myself that I didn't need them because my husband cared for me in a way they couldn't. While trying to keep it together, I put my mask back on, slid into my BMW, and drove away from these people who could not see me. What was wrong with their eyes? Didn't they know that I wasn't on the struggle bus? I didn't want money from them (it didn't look like they had any); I just wanted that thing that would fill this hole.

At this point, I was angry that I had not forced the issue of having a blood test to prove who was whom. I just wanted to connect with my people. I just wanted to know if I acted like someone from his family. Does nature prove to us who we are? I would not know, and disappointment was an understatement, but I did some praying and soul searching to resolve my unresolved issue with a person I could no longer speak with. I wrote a letter to him. I addressed it. I burned it and repeated to myself daily that I forgave him. I believed that it was all gone. I had conquered the hole, and "it" was no longer going to rule me.

It is interesting that even when you believe that situations are fixed within you, they can pop back up when you least expect them. We repeat to ourselves sayings like, "Old things are passed away, and all things have become new." This is true, but when we put the things that need to be healed in cute little boxes and sit them on the shelf, they are just like a jack-in-the-box that will pop open eventually. I thought that I was healed. However, I had just put a mask on the pain that still resided and had just gone deeper. It was no longer surface pain.

Fast forward to this year: I turned 50 and have been doing some soul work because the pandemic brought up all kinds of stuff that had been growing and festering on the bottom of the pond that is my life. I wanted to make sure that I didn't drag junk that needs to die any further into my year of jubilee, so I became actively engaged in doing soul work. Many of us don't like to do this kind of work because it is messy and takes the bows off of those pretty little packages we use to hide our mess.

My most significant breakthrough came in a weekly Bible study that I did with ladies I did not even know. I was going through becoming a fitness instructor, and this particular program overlays scripture on the whole concept of getting your body right. If you know me, I was a little skeptical of the entire concept and am not a person who loves to work out. Run for what? Yet, I felt a call to be a part. Over those nine weeks, we studied Nehemiah and all of his issues as he rebuilt the walls. I was not unfamiliar with Nehemiah, but I had never looked at Nehemiah from this vantage point. As we read and shared each week, God was allowing me to take off another layer of the cocoon I had allowed myself to be wrapped in. It was also during this time that my daddy hole popped back open.

I was sitting in the tub when an overwhelming sadness came upon me. I started talking to God about how I had missed out on having a father and how this thing always seemed to drag me down. Just like we were talking, I could hear him say, "So what?" Excuse me? I am struggling, and you said, "So what?" He went on to ask me, "What in the world did you miss out on? You had beautiful men in your life who were placed strategically at the points you needed each of them. No, they were not your daddy, but they planted the seeds necessary for you to be the powerful daughter I have called you to be. I am your Father, and don't you ever forget that. Earthly parents are there to bring you into the earth, but I am there to orchestrate this life that comes from me." "Wow" is all I could say. God just done checked me with a, "Michelle, I am Your Father." No, I am not Luke Skywalker, but I did need that reminder. I believe that was the beginning of what is such a beautiful thing that is now growing in the spot that used to be my hole.

Jeremiah 18:3-4, KJV says, *Then I went down to the potter's house, and, behold, he wrought a work on the wheels. And the vessel that he made of clay was marred in the hand of the potter: so he made it again another vessel, as seemed good to the potter to make it.*

Right there in the tub, my Father was showing me that I had been marred in the hands of people, but he was making me again, another.

If you read the scripture further, in verse five it asks, "Can't I do with you as this potter?" As I began to cry, I said, "Yes. Make me again, another." The enemy will make you and me believe that we can never get past our past, but that is a bald-faced lie. It is time to come out of that cocoon. Sister, you have been called for such a time as this, to proclaim liberty to those that are captive. It is time to come out of the shadows and live your full, authentic life.

If you struggle with unforgiveness and other unresolved issues, do this little exercise and watch God work. Write a letter to yourself. Whatever comes up, let it come up. Write it all down. At the end of the letter, write your name, then "I forgive you, and I set you free to go live your best life." Wait at least two hours. Read the letter aloud to yourself. (While you are doing this part, break up with all of the lies that have held you captive in your mind, body, and spirit.) Once you have completed this part, burn the letter. (Please be safe while doing so.) Ensure that every piece of paper is consumed by the fire so that there is nothing left. Every time the enemy brings those thoughts back, and he will, you must now call them ashes. Tell him, "Ashes don't live here anymore." Come on, sis, the enemy talks to you; talk back to him. This is the year to close that dad-sized hole for good.

Deborah V. Burrus is a highly motivated author, teacher, workshop presenter, who has dedicated her life to serving the people of God with love, integrity, and transparency. As a philanthropic pastoral leader, Deborah has an empathic and influential impact on people who have been victimized by the negative issues of life through her ability to show compassion, give guidance, and promote healing to the wounded at heart.

Deborah has traveled to many places, helping people to understand that they can be healed from the hurts of their past. Her mantra is "Your Heart Matters", Helping the Hurting, Healing the Broken. She currently serves as Senior Pastor of Restoration Outreach Center Baltimore Maryland, where she is fulfilling God's mission for her life. She is a lifelong learner who spends her time pursuing certificates and degrees and has earned a Doctor of Ministry as a Clinical Pastoral Counselor and Certified Master Life Coach. She is also the author of "When Women Weep" a message of inspiration for the wounded at heart.

Deborah can be heard weekly on the Heart Matters Internet Radio Show broadcast where she discusses pertinent issues that affect our spiritual wellness and growth. She loves spending quality time with her husband, children and grandchildren, where she can laugh, relax and enjoy life. Once you meet her, you will immediately experience the love that God has given her for all mankind.

HEART MATTERS
Deborah Burrus

The heart is the most important organ of the human body. Without its function, a person will cease to exist. God created man with a pure heart, in His image and likeness. He created man to feel the emotions of life, yet without sin.

The heart is virtually unsearchable to human beings. No one can fully understand the heart of another person and no one can fully understand his/her own heart either. Only God can plumb the depths of our hearts and render an accurate verdict as to what He finds there. This is a story about how my heart had become broken and damaged by my loss of who I was. My heart had become broken into what seemed like a million pieces. Every time I tried to fix it, it only got worse. Discovering that something is wrong with you is difficult. I had plans, I had dreams, I knew who I wanted to be. My desire as a child was to grow up and become a schoolteacher. I watched my teachers and practiced standing with the pointer or writing on chalkboards. I played school every day. I loved the suits and high heels they wore and the briefcases they carried. One day that was going to be me. That was my plan.

All of that changed when I became a teenage mother. I remember my grandmother crying when she found out, and I couldn't understand why. Little did I realize how things would change in my life. My focus was now on a child that I was clueless about raising. The good thing was that I had a great support system that made sure I finished school, but I lost sight of who I was or had planned to become. A teenage mom doesn't think like a mature woman. Who was I? What happened to my identity?

Identity is defined as the distinguishing character or personality of an individual. Keyword: distinguishing character. Teenage pregnancy had become my identity. Even though it should not have stopped anything I had planned on doing, it did. I was no longer sure of myself. I developed low self-esteem. I didn't love myself anymore, so it became easy for me to be used and abused. I began to live a life of pretending. I pretended to be happy, but I was empty inside. I labeled myself as a bad girl because of what I had allowed. My baby's father, who became my husband, was supportive, but this was about my feelings toward me.

Losing sight of who you are will cause you to feel like you are trapped in someone else's body. At least this was how I felt. You want to be free but don't know how to get free. I tried to cover my feelings by staying active and being a part of the crowd. I no longer thought about a career so I began to work without a clear plan in sight. I just wanted to fit in so I would not think about how disappointed I was in myself. Notice I said disappointed in myself. Nobody was saying things about me; this was all in my head. I was really messed up in my head and in my heart. I sought out a therapist who tried to help but I wouldn't stick with the process. I ran from my feelings. Even after marriage I continued to run from my feelings. I became a people pleaser. All I wanted was for people to like me. What was it that happened to me that was so terrible I could not face? During this time, I would cry a lot. People would see me, and they thought I had it all together, but they did not know how I felt on the inside. I was in a downward-spiraling condition that I did not believe I could recover from. Suicide was even part of my thought processes. I went back to therapy and began to take medication. The medicine helped, but if you do not confront what is really going on you will never get well. I wanted to be healed but there were some things I had to learn. I was in pain. I felt like there was a hole in my heart and I could not fix it. It is amazing how one situation can change your life in such a damaging way that you feel like you will never get back on the right track.

What happened to me was not much different from the same thing happening to someone else. It is all in how we process things. I was brought up to believe that you could take a licking and keep on ticking. I was taught to be strong, to be courageous and to stand up for myself. So that is what I did when I was around people. But that was not how I was when I was by myself. I felt alone and empty inside. I began to seek God in a way that I had not done before. I needed to change because it was eating me up inside. God revealed to me that what I was experiencing was a lack of love for myself, unforgiveness and fear. This is what was causing my heart to feel damaged and broken. Once my problems were identified I began to see myself as broken, but I could be healed. I began to ask the question, "Why do I not love me?" Love is that beautiful gift from God that you have to give to yourself. You can love others but if you do not love yourself, you will never experience the joys of life. I stopped loving myself when I believed people were disappointed with me. I stopped loving me when I felt that I did not measure up. I stopped loving me when I no longer felt I could look in the mirror because I did not like what I saw. The problem with all of this was that it was in my head. Nobody was judging me but me. God showed me that if I learned to accept responsibility for my actions, they would no longer be staring me in the face. He also showed me that who I am was not determined by the mistakes I made. Learning the true meaning of love is one of the greatest joys you can experience. The love I speak of is not based on how you feel about me or how I feel about you, but how God feels about us. His love is the greatest love of all.

When I discovered how much God loves me, my perspective on life changed. God's love is unconditional. Our love, however, is usually conditional and is based on how other people behave toward us. It is predicated upon familiarity and direct or indirect interaction. As I studied God's love, I learned that nothing could separate me from His love. His love is immutable; it does not change. His love is forgiving, caring and unconditional. God wants you to know that there is nothing that you have done that is so terrible that it will keep Him from loving you when you accept Him. For me this meant everything. I was now on my way to bigger and better things. But I had to deal with that unforgiveness and fear if I really wanted to be better.

Forgiveness was not an easy area for me to handle. After all, we assume that if we do not think about those areas of our lives that have caused undue pain they will go away. I did not know my past had so adversely affected my life. While I pretended to be okay, I was reminded of the warning signs that something was dreadfully wrong. Those warning signs were reflected in my attitude about myself. I became bitter and a people pleaser. Lack of self-esteem and low self-worth had become my friends. I did what I could to survive, but my life was not about me. I allowed others to make my choices. I settled and did not strive for what I wanted. I existed and that was about it. I followed the crowd's lead. I did not see a way out of this lifestyle and thought it must have been my punishment.

All it took was for me to pray to God and ask God for forgiveness for all the wrong I had ever done and for me to forgive all who had wronged me. "Lord, I forgive" is simple to say but hard to do. One of the greatest lessons I have learned is that cleansing comes from forgiveness (1 John 1:9). God cleansed me and made me new.

The final thing in this process that I had to overcome was fear. Change is fearful. I had to learn how to walk in my real identity and be my true, authentic self. Losing sight of who you were intended to become can be challenging. Fear had kept me from pursuing my dreams and goals. To overcome this, I placed my focus on reading self-help books and continuing my therapy. One book that was a real asset to my healing process, was *You Can Heal Your Life* by Louise Hay. I learned that fear was only an emotion, and it did not come from God. As I planned my future, fear began to dissipate. I discovered that those dreams and aspirations had never left me but had only laid dormant on the inside of me waiting to be reclaimed. It was time to break up the fallow ground. "Sow to yourselves in righteousness, reap in mercy; break up your fallow ground: for it is time to seek the Lord, till he come and rain righteousness upon you." (Hosea 10:12, KJV)

Fallow ground is that which has been plowed but not sown; it is ground not in use – idle ground crusted over and hardened until it needs to be broken up again to receive the seed. We must break up the ground of our hearts and yield them to God. If I wanted righteousness to rain upon me, I had to break up the fallow ground.

I discovered that my feelings did not come from how I felt about people but how I felt about myself. I had picked up evil habits along the way which were weeds growing around my heart. This kept me in a whirlwind of uncertainty, pain and anguish. I had been sowing seeds of discord where there should have been seeds of righteousness. The feeling of not being good enough had taken over. I discovered I was using the wrong fertilizer. Instead of sowing spiritual seeds of words of endless possibilities, I was sowing words of extreme negativity.

One of the most damaging things you can do to yourself is to not accept who you are. God knew what He was doing when He created you. Accepting who you are is learning to see what God sees. You have been fearfully and wonderfully made and there is nothing you can do to change that. You don't have to live up to anyone's standards. Breaking that fallow ground meant taking a long look in the mirror. Not a glance, but a long look. I begin to look at the imperfections, not in my face but in my soul and in my spirit. When I looked into my soul – the seat of my emotions – I found that I was one hot mess. My emotions were all over the Richter scale. Emotions can be like whirlwinds, ever turning, trying to find a place to land. My emotions dictated my life. Do not live your life based on how you feel. Feelings are unpredictable. We have all made decisions based on how we felt, and some of those decisions were not good ones. Emotions control our thinking, behavior, and actions. God gave us emotions as part of our souls, but our whole lives should not revolve around the impulses of our emotions.

What is in your heart can be evidenced in your emotions. Your heart reveals when you are afraid, when you are discouraged, when you are sad or in need of comfort, when you feel convicted of sin and when you are rejoicing. My emotions consisted of negative feelings about who I was instead of realizing all God had created me to be. I needed to take my feelings to the cross and allow the Holy Spirit to teach me that although they were a part of me, they did not have to control me. God had to destroy the fiery nature of my emotions with its confusion, and subject it totally to spiritual authority. It is the cross of Jesus Christ that gets rid of the confusion of our emotions. When God takes control, you understand what being balanced is all about.

My mind had me singing Frank Sinatra's song, "I did it my way." I wanted to be loved but I did not love myself. I thought it took people to make you happy. Boy, was I wrong. Some people believe happiness comes through experiences of pleasure, i.e., having fun at a party, the thrill of passion and sex, a night out on the town, or a fine dinner – you get the picture. Our happiness changes day by day, depending on the situation. If we are not careful, we will find ourselves seekers of pleasure, thinking that it is happiness. Chasing pleasure is not happiness. Kenneth Benjamin describes happiness as the feeling you get when your life fulfills your needs. Happiness comes when you feel satisfied and fulfilled. For me, fulfillment became my happiness.

I also went through the process of learning to love me. I did not think I was good enough. No one said it to me, but it was what I thought. I had to learn that each of us must live the life God created for us and not compare it to someone else's.

Facing the fact that I did not love myself was hard. The enemy has a way of making you feel bad about yourself by focusing on your imperfections, When I looked at myself, I saw rejection, doubt, and fear. I wanted to be like other people. I discovered I did not know how to love me. Loving yourself is developing an attitude of self-respect, protecting your heart, and personally caring for your needs. I began to treat myself to flowers, go to a restaurant and enjoy a meal alone, and invested in ways to care for me personally, like bubble baths, massages, facials and shopping just because.

This is the only dependable way to create love in your own life that you can share with others. I discovered ways of letting go of the past so I could live better in the present. Defining myself by what I had accomplished rather than what I had not served as a catapult to get me where I needed to be.

The Bible tells us to love our neighbors as ourselves (Leviticus 19:8). We talk about the importance of loving our neighbor, but rarely talk about loving ourselves in the same manner we love them. I cannot in all fairness love my neighbor if I do not love myself. If I love me, I should want to take care of me. I have found it easier to take care of other people's problems and help them find a solution than to take care of my own personal needs. When I began to break up the fallow pieces of my heart, I noticed how peaceful my life was becoming. I was no longer just working; I was focused on my career, which began to do quite well. God was showing me that everything in my life has a purpose and it was working for my good.

Another lesson I have learned through all of this is to never give up on you. You have what it takes to make it in this life. Your obstacles, hurdles, disappointments, and setbacks are all a part of God's plan. Everything is working together for your good. Don't allow anyone or anything to keep you from evolving into God's chosen vessel. I now know who I am. The young woman who lost sight of her identity is now living a life of gratitude and fulfillment. I have gone back to school and earned a bachelor's degree in theology. I also became a licensed clinical pastoral counselor, a certified life coach, and a senior pastor of a local church. I became successful in my secular job and have now retired, loving who I have become. I am no longer ashamed of who I am or what I did. I live each day to the fullest, recognizing that I was not put here by accident. I have work to do. It is now my time to use what I have learned to share and help others to do likewise. I am nowhere near finished. I am who God created me to be, with all my imperfections. Most importantly, I am in love with me, and I know who I am. Always remember, your heart matters.

Ashley Stallings-Small was born with a purpose and designed for greatness. The middle of three strong-willed and talented children, her parents instilled in her the belief that any goal is attainable. At the tender age of nineteen, she had a baby and the roller coaster of life began. Her faith, leadership, and pure emotions have been exposed, changed, and redesigned over these last seven years.

Ashley is grateful for all the daggers thrown her way because they allowed her to gain a new sense of self. She is a woman of strength, beauty, class, and restraint. Now she is putting herself and her son back in the potter's hands. Each individual day (and the days since then) she had her principles tried and tested by the enemy (through people and circumstances) but, God has stayed faithful throughout.

Ashley's belief in the most high led her to become the first in her family to achieve a college degree. Ashley is currently teaching and obtaining her PhD in Special Education.

PROSPERING IN HARD TIMES

Ashley Stallings-Small

What do you do when pain and purpose intermix? Pain, anger, turmoil, and defeat were all staring me in the face as I listened to the nurse at Planned Parenthood tell me I was six weeks pregnant. I was shocked—too shocked to even respond to her. I walked out of the exam room and back into my friend's car and headed back to my college dorm room. I could sense the disappointment family and friends would have in me and the disgust I had in myself. Only 19, I saw my whole life come to a complete stop. Years of self-doubt and self-expression spilled into all of my conversations.

I finally mustered enough courage to call home to be greeted by a mother, who received word from the Lord that I was pregnant. God left room for no surprises. He protected me in my weakest moment.

I spent the last semester of my freshman year concealing a pregnancy that I never wanted. I believed God was punishing me for exploring every avenue available to me. Throughout my pregnancy I existed solely as a host mother to bring a life into the world. I lost myself, my identity, and I made a vow to myself that I would achieve everything the naysayers told me I never would. This caused a lot of unnecessary stress and added pressure that never was assigned to me but I chose to carry because I believed it was owed to me. I felt just like that commercial with the paper smiley face posted over the woman's face in every photo. I felt like I was drowning while everyone watched with popcorn and streamers. I chose to rest in my emotions because they were the only thing I could control. I gave birth to my son alone in a hospital room and I thought my pain would finally end. I mean, I did what everyone wanted me to do. I birthed the kid into the world; now my life could go back to normal, right? Wrong.

I began to pray in defeat for God to either take me out of this or find some way to ease the pain. As my son got bigger the decision making began to get worse. Court cases, minimum wage and school assignments took over my life. I felt like every day I woke up, I fought to do the same the next day. I hoped tomorrow I would make it out or I just would not wake up. The worst part was I felt like God did not care either way. I felt extremely defeated. I finally secured a job and because it was in the fast-food industry, I was only able to make $7.25 an hour, which would not allow me to take care of myself or my son. So I moved myself into income-based housing just so we could live on our own. It was the easiest thing to do because I had family who lived out there. So the rental place decided that I would be a good fit. I spent about a year and a half at that job working between 10 and 15 hours a week because the manager denied me more hours. During this time, I was also cycling in and out of various medical programs trying to solidify a way to make a decent wage to support my household. Faith was literally the size of a mustard seed. I depended on God for every breath. Well, God made a way for not only my son to get into a preschool program but also for me to begin my Associate's degree. Because I already completed a year at the college that I was attending before I got pregnant, I only had to complete a total of 30 credits.

Praise God, because it could've gone a different way. I entered into my program at a time when online education was fairly new but I knew that this was the only direction I could go in and I had to take drastic measures in order to be successful. God allowed for me to be placed in the right hands the entire time that I was in school. With God's grace and mercy, I was able to complete my Associate's degree in one year. With a degree I was able to apply for a job in education and finally was able to leave that other job and free up my weekends. This allowed me to spend more time with my son, and I would begin working on my Bachelor's degree.

My life was getting better. I was beginning to snap out of the funk that came along with the pandemic and poverty that had become my life from the ages of 19 to 24. At around 23 years old I decided that my next adventure would be for me to get a car and teach myself how to drive. I'd never been behind the wheel and had no experience with cars or buying cars, so I decided the smartest thing to do was to look on Craigslist and purchase a car from there. Around the same time my apartment had been flooded out and we were staying in a hotel until the complex could basically restructure our entire bottom unit. I found a 91 Oldsmobile for $1000 on Craigslist and I used my tax return to buy it. The man I bought it from used to own a car dealership so he took really good care of it. Mind you, I had never been behind the wheel so when he left I snail-drove the car from one hotel parking lot to my hotel parking lot. It was by God's grace that I was even able to park the car the correct way. Moving into the hotel showed me that I could rekindle my relationship with God. I drove the car for about two days before I decided it was time for me to go to the DMV to take my driver's test. On my way to the DMV office, I decided it was a good idea to drop my son off at daycare. While I was driving, I tried to make a narrow U-turn on a small street but instead of pressing the brake to slow the car down as I was making the turn, I pressed the accelerator and we went through a couple of bushes and a pole and stopped an inch short of a gas station building. We made so much noise when the car jerked back that the cashier inside ran out to see what the commotion was. God's protecting angels made sure that we didn't hit a car and that no car hit us within that intersection. It's by God saving grace that we are even here to this day. When the officer arrived, he allowed me to take my son back to the hotel, which was only about 500 feet away from where we got into the accident. He gave me a ticket and he allowed me to go on about my day.

I could've allowed that moment to harden me from ever wanting to drive again but I knew that God saving me meant that there were other opportunities for me. So back I went through Craigslist to find another car and found a 2002 Ford explorer. It also cost $1000 but with this car I received my license. I'll never forget that rainy day in December. Right before I had to go to work at a daycare center, I drove myself to the DMV and took my driving test. The lady gave me my evaluation and passed me because she said the rain caused me to make mistakes. This was the biggest accomplishment I'd ever made in my 24 years because this was simply done on merit. No family helped me; nobody taught me—I did this with God's help alone. I paid for six driving classes and only received two and never heard back from the man who was supposed to help me with the driving, but the Lord is good.

By the time I went to court I had my license and left the court room only owing the court fees and the amount of money that it cost to fix the pole, because it was public property. When I tell people this part of my life, they are so astounded by how I was not given any jail time or heavier consequences because of me driving without having a license and that we were protected and walked out of the accident with not a scratch or a scar. This situation will always be a reminder to me of the grace of God and his presence in situations near and far.

Being born and raised in the church I knew that Sundays were for church. So one Sunday, after watching a revival and crying my eyes out, I decided to wake up and find the first church with its door open. God ordained every decision that I made that day because he allowed me to walk into a church that accepted me and my child as well as intentionally wanted us to grow in the spirit. I'd never been around people who physically wanted to help you just because it was the right thing to do. And because I'd never been exposed to this kind of love, I ran from it. I hid from it for a long time. Whenever I was called upon, I would always decide to retreat and hide within myself. I struggled with believing that God wanted to use someone whose plan did not work out the way they expected it to. But God had other plans for me. We finally got back into our apartment and I had to start from zero. God provided a way for me to not only be gifted with new furniture but also better furniture than what I had lost in the flood.

Because I was not flourishing as much as expected in Virginia, I decided that I needed to change. I cried my eyes out one night and told God that I needed a fresh start and no matter where He sent me, I was going to go. I started to apply for jobs all over the seven cities in the Carolinas. I got a call from one of the childcare providers in North Carolina. I got this through my cousin. The lady wanted me to meet her in North Carolina at 8 AM. That was three hours away from where I lived and in order to do that, we had to leave at around 4 AM. I thought it would be easy because she was there the whole way, but she pushed me to do exceedingly above what I was comfortable with and made me drive the entire three hours, breaking my fear of highways and byways.

God was purposely positioning me in ways to show me that my strength did not lie in other people or in situations, but if I always relied on Him, strength would come. I couldn't be so bogged down with a specific way that I ignored the way maker.

I arrived at the job, crushed the interview and walked away with an offer. The only issue was, we did not have a place to stay while we were there. My mind told me to get a hotel room and stay there for two weeks until I received my first paycheck. I did not want to open my mouth and let anyone else know what was going on but God had a ram in the bush.

My uncle, who I had not communicated with for a year, called me and asked me what I was up to. I told him that I received a new job in North Carolina and Mia and I were going to move that next week so I could be paid for my job. He asked me about my location and where the job was. I told him and he asked who it was. I didn't have an answer for him. He told me he'd call me back. When he did call me back, he not only had a place for us to stay but we were able to stay there rent free. Again, the Lord showed His providing hand when I was willing to make the move and say hey, however the provision comes, wherever it comes from, I'm going in this direction because I know you're pulling me here. Later that week I packed up my 2002 Honda accord with all of my son's and my belongings that we could take with us and drove up to Raleigh, North Carolina to start a new life. When I got there, I was accustomed to doing everything alone and I was brought into a family that I hadn't communicated with in a while. God used those three years to flourish me and to allow me to understand that greater and better for me and my son did not mean that I was losing myself or that I had to give up anything.

Throughout this whole journey I was able to keep myself in school. After my Associate's degree I went directly into my Bachelor's degree at a different school and was able to complete that in two years. I was going to be done with school because I felt like this degree would give me the certification that I needed to teach and I would be happy making a minimum living on an educated salary. But it just wasn't enough. God opened up dreams and visions in me that I allowed to be dormant throughout this process in this transition. I decided to go for my Master's degree to prove to myself and those around me that having a child at an early age did not disqualify me from achieving any goal. The school I entered was introduced to me through a co-teacher for their teacher certification program. I attended their classes and liked it so much that I decided to join their newly formed Special Education Master's program. Being part of the founding class came with its own set of gifts and transitions. I felt like a guinea pig in some situations because there was no blueprint to fashion myself for school. We were the first class to ever try out the schedule, try out the curriculum, or even enroll in the program. Being one of two students in a program allowed me to fine-tune all of my educational work because it was like I had personal instructors for every subject.

My instructors showed me that anything was possible. They took the time to sit with me to make sure they understood what kind of teacher I wanted to be. The feedback was intentional and they really showed me how an educational leader was supposed to conduct themselves. I didn't know it at the time but God was giving me several examples of how to conduct myself in a professional work environment. From then on, I decided that there were no gaps that could keep me from living the life that God had ordained for me. After spending two years in North Carolina, I decided to go where God had originally told me: New York City. This place scared the bananas out of me because of everything that I thought I knew about it. I didn't think I was quite ready to experience the greatness that I thought New York City was. Even though I had come out of my depression I still saw myself as surviving life with minimal joy instead of thriving in life with absolute joy. But God was getting ready to change that.

When I moved to New York City God blessed me to be in a safe space where I could make financial as well as life decisions that might not have been the smartest, but I was protected from any ill will. He again led me to a place of favor where if I had allowed my fears to continue to stop me, I would have never been able to be open. Living in New York allowed me to finally break the shells that had attached themselves around my heart, my mind and my spirit. I no longer considered myself less than because I knew I was worth more and I didn't make apologies for being worth more. No matter how long or short I have been in a place, God's intentionality kept me from shattering into a million pieces. He used each and every opportunity to build trust and accountability in my life.

When I got to New York I assumed that everything would be better. And for a while it was because I chose to make intentional choices to make it better. I discovered a lot about myself in the second move. I felt more freedom than ever and felt ready to take over the world. Looking back, I thank God for his ability to know the end from the beginning because he structured every experience for me to use what I learned in the previous session to my advantage. I didn't have to carry the baggage of my past into the new session but I could carry the experience. The experience in my new session showed me how to save money, budget for existence, and understand what I liked and didn't like in relationships. The lessons of the past strengthened me for the present.

Now that I am an official New Yorker, I see how I needed everything I experienced. Without the previous situations, no matter how hard they were, I would not have been able to stand firm in anything. I would blow side to side depending on which way the wind blew and I would not be able to stand firm in any of my decisions. I would be cowardly in my career as well as in my personal life. My prayers are still constantly "God, why?" and filled with "God, when?" instead of targeting my prayers toward things that matter. This experience helped me to resolve the fact that God is on my side and because He is on my side no other help is necessary. I tried help from other people. They let me down. I tried help from substances. They let me down. I tried help from fornication. It left me empty and barren. I tried running from my calling and it showed up anyway.

Everything was going well until the 2020 pandemic shifted my ability to control. I felt the lesson in my whole situation was how to organize, but the real lesson was in trust. My life flipped from five days a week hustling and bustling to seven days a week not knowing what direction life was going in. Not only did I have to flip my daily schedule to working over a computer that cared nothing about me, but I had to also flip my son's schedule to a remote learning environment. Budget cuts, staff meetings, and making videos took over my entire life. I began to freak out because I felt my momentum leaving and fear setting in. Every week we would get a new instruction and I went into another clinical depression. This time it showed up in becoming an overachiever. I threw myself into my PhD program and started taking double and sometimes triple the classes to avoid reality. I started reliving past experiences in a new season.

Here's what I learned that kept me throughout the entire process: 1) Be authentic in your feelings. God can handle it and you are worth the truth. 2) Prayer throughout strengthens you in it. Allow your prayer life to grow at your pace and not others'. 3) Progress does not mean perfection. Step by step your way through your journey. 4) Your calling is going to find you, whether or not you accept the call. Answer and walk in it. 5) Just because a mistake is made it doesn't disqualify you from bigger and better things.

Tyla Yancey, mentor, empowerment coach, and speaker, is passionate about empowering women to reach higher heights. She is the founder of Envisions Empowerment Group and is currently building her coaching practice. One of her greatest accomplishments was overcoming the challenges of teenage motherhood and the stigmas that come with the role. Despite obstacles, she went on to earn three degrees while raising her two children as a single mother.

Tyla is an analyst within the Federal Government and has been writing and publishing policies, procedures, and technical decisions for over 15 years. As she climbed her ladder of success, she lived by the words of Taoist philosopher Chuang Tzu "Just when the caterpillar thought the world was over, it became a butterfly." Tyla sees herself as that caterpillar. She approaches every challenge as an opportunity for change, to spread her wings and fly higher, representing the beautiful butterfly she has become.

MORE THAN A CONQUEROR

Tyla Yancey

> *"Yet in all things we are more than conquerors*
> *through Him who loved us."*
> Romans 8:37, NKJV

Who am I? I am a product of my choices. Society has yelled out to me on many occasions that we are a product of our environment and circumstances. However, this statement has been proven to be untrue on many levels. Yes, I have made choices based on my environment or circumstances. But in many instances my environment and circumstances were a product of said choices—life choices. I faced situations of serious difficulty, survived moments of distress and indiscretion, and overcame what may be viewed as some serious misfortune. Nonetheless, through it all I learned that I have the power to more than overcome any setback or challenge that arises on my path. My struggles could not and would not define who I am. Instead, whether I allowed my struggles to affect my life did. Albert Einstein said it best: "Adversity introduces a man to himself." As such, adversity introduced me to the woman I look at in the mirror and identify as More Than a Conqueror!

Women have been faced with adversity since the beginning of time and have been taught how to be strong and survive--*ALONE*. I have been taught no different and mastered it! Being a young black girl raised by a single mother in low-income housing, I was taught that survival was the key to life. And did I mention that the best way to do this was alone? This was far from the truth and life's lessons have taught me that I have never walked and will never walk alone.

At the age of three, I became a "fatherless" child. Although I longed to be a daddy's girl, I learned to appreciate having a mother who provided everything she thought was necessary for my growth and security. What she did not know is what I needed most to feel secure and loved was truth, honesty, and emotional support. I did not have everything I wanted; but I had everything I needed to "survive." I became an outstanding scholar in grade school and excelled without an adult overseeing my schoolwork or time. I had free range while my mother was out "making ends meet." Nonetheless, I had no desire to creep off and indulge in drugs, sex, and pregnancy even though the opportunities were present, and my peers were heavily involved in these activities at a very young age. I was beginning to learn to "survive" and to do so all on my own. After all, my mother told me that I came into this world alone and needed no one to help me to "survive" through it. It was in those moments I was given permission to "do bad all by myself because I did not need anyone to help me do bad." If I had done it all on my own and failed, it was ok. Therefore, I went through life thinking that doing it on my own and being successful was the only way and expecting support was living beyond expectation. The reality that I quickly learned was that I did need God, support, and a help mate. Through this experience, I was slowly but surely introduced to the adversities of my childhood—**fatherlessness,**

lack of emotional attachment, lack of positive guidance, poverty, and sexual abuse.

By high school, I had my focus on one thing and one thing only—survival. I had a very skewed view of what that meant and no idea of how to accomplish my newfound goal of surviving. My thought—if I graduate on time and obtain a job, it will help me survive adulthood. Although I attended a college preparatory high school, I thought college was out of my reach. I knew no one who had attended college and it was never discussed in my home. Among my peers, I pretended to apply for colleges in my 12th grade year but never did one application. I had no idea how college would play out financially and was fearful of asking any questions. I simply wrote it off and continued with my mind set on finding a way to survive. However, four months before graduation, I became pregnant. I gave birth to my first child five months after graduating from high school and four months after my 18th birthday. I was introduced to the first adversity in my young adult life—**teenage motherhood**.

On November 14, 1988, I became a mother. Although I was legally an adult, I was a teenager who was trying to figure out how to survive alone and now had to do it for someone else—her child. Although my son's father was still in our lives, the circumstances were less than ideal. We were both young and still had no idea where life was taking us. With the help of my middle sister, I was offered the opportunity to move into a low-income home to start a life for my child. His father came along and adulting began, abruptly. Two months later, I sat in an employment agency and flipped through a three-inch-thick binder one page at a time. I was in search of something that could become a career but had no clue what that would be. This led me to a six-month long medical and legal transcription certification program. Again, I was looking for a way to survive. Little did I know, this program would be a pivotal point in my life.

In February 1989, I started the certification program and was excelling swiftly. I was advised that I would be given the opportunity for job placement after completing four months instead of six. One month later my instructor left the program, and I was introduced to "the typing teacher." Unbeknownst to me, she was intrigued by my drive. After she was offered a position at another company as a word-processing manager, she called the school and requested a few students for an interview for a position. I was one and I was hired. It was more than exciting to start my first job with benefits. But what then happened to my life was never expected. My success was not welcomed in my home. I met new people and started exploring who I was becoming. This newfound lifestyle was met by a now "somewhat" abusive relationship and home life. After all, didn't everyone fuss and fight? Didn't that mean that he cared about me a lot? This was not real abuse. Or was it?

Despite the abusive behavior, I bought a house and married my son's father at the age of 21. What I neglected to share earlier in this story is that I was baptized when I was pregnant with my son. However, I was unsure of what it really meant. My childhood lacked spiritual and religious teaching beyond the Lord's prayer and occasionally attending church with my grandmother and oldest sister. During my pregnancy, I was introduced to sin and forgiveness. I repented, was baptized, and tried to live "right." Although I was not very knowledgeable, I knew that we were living in sin since we were not married. We had a conversation, attended pre-marital counseling with the minister of our church, and were married four weeks later. Seven months after our wedding, I became pregnant with our second child. At the age of 22, I gave birth to a baby girl on October 16, 1992.

From 1992 through 1997, I lived in an abusive marriage. I hid it well. It started off emotionally and verbally abusive and slowly became more and more physical. I kept telling myself that it wasn't that bad because I was not punched and never had bruises. He *only* dragged me down the steps every so often was the way I thought of it. And the time the blood ran down my face was *only* because I was cut on my scalp from the glass that ricocheted off the wall when he threw the plate that slightly missed my head. *I'm a survivor; I can get through this.* He had choked me on numerous occasions, crashed my car with me in it, sped through a stockade fence with me standing on the other side, and thrown a crowbar through my car window. None of it broke me, so I *thought,* and I was going to be o.k. After all, I just wanted a man to love me. This one had been here with me for 11 years, so it had to be love. Right? No one in my life stuck around that long. Allow me to introduce the second adversity of my adult life—**Domestic Violence**.

Reality check! The abuse did break me. It broke my spirit, attacked my drive for success, and crippled my self-esteem. I no longer wanted to survive. I was co-existing. I worked, slowly retreated from friends and family, and became depressed. I watched my children respond to the negative environment and felt trapped because I did not know how to help them. At times I felt this was all I was worth. During this phase, I met more adversities in my adult life—**depression and self-doubt**. I thought I would never get out. But God stepped in! Or did He?

Some would recognize the day I walked away from the abuse as the pivotal point in my life, but I introduced you to what I recognize as the pivotal point in my life back in 1989. Choosing to start the word-processing certification program led me to "the typing teacher." It was "the typing teacher" who took me under her wing and mentored me into the woman I am today. It was "the typing teacher" who introduced me to the "ride or die friend" who shared travel expenses with me so that I could get my son to daycare to keep my job. It was "the typing teacher" and the "ride or die friend" who showed up, without hesitancy, with a box of trash bags to move me out of my abusive situation. In April 1996, I left my abusive marriage and three months before my 27th birthday I filed for a divorce. It was that "ride or die friend" who shared parenting duties with me as I tackled single motherhood. She even took time from work to assist when my daughter had an eye injury resulting in seeing an ophthalmologist *every day* for two weeks. At that moment, I met the rest of my adult adversities—**divorce and single motherhood**.

My life changed drastically. But guess what? I SURVIVED IT! I used all those survival tactics that got me here. At least that is how I thought I got here. I taught myself to master anything that I needed to do to survive in a single income household. If something was broken, I learned to fix it. When the alternator in the car went up, I learned to change it. When we needed furniture, I bought wood and made it. I even enrolled in college without having a babysitter and my children attended with me. I did what I had to do and obtained three degrees, enhanced my career, married the love of my life, found out I never knew how love felt, felt TRUE LOVE, realized I did not know how to love, learned how to GIVE LOVE, had amazing grandkids, experienced real happiness for the first time, and bought my dream house. I am a TRUE SURVIVOR—that is how I referred to myself.

Then I woke up!

To survive has been defined as being able to "continue to live or exist in spite of danger or hardship." Throughout life's storms, I was faced with hardship, trials, tribulations, distress, and persecution. After it all, I still lived. To live is to remain alive. Being alive is simply awaking each day, breathing, and functioning. I did this. But was it enough? I was going through life surviving and was proud of it. One day I opened my eyes and realized that I was living but deserved to thrive. I was allowing my past circumstances to dictate my actions and reactions, hence, making me a survivor. At that moment I realized that I must *survive*, but while surviving, I must thrive.

I succeeded in dealing with my tribulations and overcame the adversaries. Therefore, I am not a survivor, I am an overcomer. I am a conqueror. After all, conquerors are people who conquer or overcome an adversary. As I overcame adversities the lessons came abundantly. Butterflies cannot fly without going through the fight of coming out of the cocoon. The wings are strengthened from pushing through its life. I had become that butterfly. I was a caterpillar that climbed on top of each stone thrown in my path until I could see beyond my circumstances. And just as that caterpillar thought life was over, she became a butterfly and flew above it all. I am more than a conqueror. Not only did I overcome the adversity, but I also learned how to deal with what life has brought since then and will bring in my path.

How did I get here? Remember, God stepped in! Or did He? When I did not know God was there, He kept me. With little adult supervision, my world could have been destined for demise. But He had a plan! In my heart, I had a curfew when I went in the house when the lights came on. In my soul, someone would find out if I followed friends to neighborhoods that could have led to unfathomable desires. In my mind, someone would check my schoolwork or make sure I actually attended class. But most importantly, in my spirit, He did. Romans 8:35-36, KJV reads, "Who shall separate us from the love of Christ? Shall tribulation, or distress, or persecution, or famine, or nakedness, or peril, or sword? For Your sake we are killed all day long; We are accounted as sheep for the slaughter." God did *not* step in when I could not muster up the strength to leave an abusive marriage and provide a safe environment for my children. God was there all along.

Psalms 73:26, NIV reads, "My flesh and my heart fail; But God is the strength of my heart and my portion forever." Every person I met on my path, every door that was closed and every window that was opened was placed there for me to overcome the adversities. When I had given up, God fought every battle and whispered to me to be at peace (Exodus 14:14). I refused to listen. How could I be at peace when my less than desirable tribulations continued to threaten my happiness? How could I be at peace when the memories swam in my head when I tried to forget? How could I be at peace when my children bore witness to things that would affect their lives forever? Instead, I now ask myself how I still rise and continue to grow. The answer is simple. I wanted to be loved and all along God loved me. Romans 8:37, NIV reads, "Yet in all these things we are more than conquerors through Him who loved us." Then I am reminded that rain is needed for flowers to grow. There's no more rain in this cloud. Now watch me grow and grow beautifully!

> *"The flower that blooms in adversity*
> *is the rarest and most beautiful of all."*
> – Walt Disney

It Was God Who Pulled Me Through

Some wanted to see me fall:
She won't walk; she'll get down to her knees and crawl.
How can she possibly get over that wall?
Because as you see, she's just not that tall.

Baby at 18,
Married at 21,
Then an abusive marriage leading to divorce—
Man, she's got to be done!

But when Circus entertainers want to be tall
They climb on top of stilts,
And not so tall is simply how I was built.
I didn't have stilts; instead, God, I had you.
I climbed on top of you to do what I needed to do.

Without you and the circle only you could have built around me,
My beginning could have been my end.

Yes, it was you
Who pulled me through.
I got over by standing on your shoulders.

Now a scholar who received three degrees
while being a single mother too,
Yes, I did exactly what I needed to do.
I proudly hold my head high, but I try not to boast
Because with your help, through the obstacles thrown my way,
I've grown taller than most.
So to my struggles I say grand thanks from me to you
For helping me RISE as STILL I'LL DO!

Patricia Thomas, is a wife, mother, grandmother, caregiver, entrepreneur and philanthropist, passionate about helping and serving people. She is an encourager. She shares wisdom and life experiences to support others in discovering purpose.

Patricia has served professionally in administrative and managerial capacities in corporate law, social services, and education.

As a woman of faith, she has served in various ministries in leadership, including teaching and mentoring youth.

A JOURNEY OF CAREGIVING

Patricia Thomas

In most cases the role of a caregiver is not planned and can arise suddenly due to varying medical circumstances. It can start off gradually or it can literally occur overnight.

Phase One

As I spent time with Mommy, I remember realizing that she seemed to be experiencing challenges with her memory. After seeking medical attention, my observance was confirmed. She was experiencing some dementia. Accepting this was hard, and it was actually frightening to think about. How would this play out? At the time, Mommy was living in a Senior Community that she absolutely loved. She had friends, great socialization, and she enjoyed having her own place.

The decision to take on the responsibility of a caregiver can be based on more than the physical conditions alone. The decision can be rooted in love, respect, honor, devotion, compassion and support for loved ones. Families may want to follow the tradition that has occurred in the past, and they may also feel more assured of the loved one's quality of care. If the care recipient is a parent, a child may feel that it is now their turn to take care of their parent just as they took care of them. For me, it was all of the above.

Mommy's condition did not change rapidly and that was a plus. For several months, I was able to do most things on my own, with some help from family members. As time went by, I realized that I was totally taking care of two households. Or was I? I could not have been hitting the mark at both homes. I was exhausted. I am not Super Human or Super Woman!

I had a discussion with Mommy about getting someone to come in and help with some basic day-to-day needs. The conversation did not go well. She was not interested in someone that she did not know coming into her home. She didn't feel that it was necessary and assured me that I was doing a great job. It was also true that she was still capable of doing quite a few things on her own and I am sure that she wanted to hold on to that. She may have interpreted bringing someone else in as me believing that she could no longer do things for herself. It challenged her independence. This was her home and she did have the right to say who was welcome there. I remember leaving and thinking, *What in the world am I going to do? I cannot continue to do this on my own.*

Although the idea was not well-received, I knew it was time to get some help! I was aware of the fact that this was a sensitive area. Besides me being overwhelmed, there were two other important components in this decision process. I knew that it was important for Mommy to feel that she was maintaining some degree of independence and it was also important to me that she was safe. I began to take action. I did some research and connected with the proper resources that would result in obtaining a home health-care aide to assist with some of Mommy's daily needs. Everything had been set in place for Mommy to have an aide come out but I had not made the final phone call so that someone would actually start. There was a woman who already cared for another resident in the building who was a friend of Mommy's and they interacted quite often. I had conversed with her on a few occasions, as well. I approached her one day to see if she might be interested in having another client in the building, I asked her to think about it and get back to me. After a couple of discussions, she officially became Mommy's home aide. She would come in three days a week for three hours. Mom and I both felt comfortable with her and she was glad to be there.

There are different levels of caregiving that may be taken on as it relates to the needs of the recipient. It may start with becoming roommates and assuming full responsibility for your loved one's needs. Or it may start with more frequent phone calls and home visits, attending doctor appointments, shopping, meal prep, banking and arranging for outside services. The latter is where it began for me!

I have learned that one individual cannot fulfill all the needs of the care recipient. You cannot do it alone. Let me repeat: You cannot do it alone. When the caregiver becomes overwhelmed both parties may suffer. As a caregiver it is often thought that the recipient is our main focus. This is true, but maybe not in the sense that you originally think about it. In order for a caregiver to focus on the recipient they must take care of themselves first and foremost. Self-care is an aspect of our lives that we always seem to put on the back burner. Well, it doesn't belong on the back burner; it belongs in the forefront. Self-care is a major part of the fuel we need as individuals to carry out our daily assignments, to be active in our relationships and to live a desirable level of fulfillment in all aspects of life. As we pour out to others, we must find ways to replenish ourselves. We must replenish and build ourselves up spiritually, physically, emotionally and intellectually. When we don't take care of ourselves, we may show up in ways that don't benefit us or others.

Throughout the caregiver journey there will always be a need for others to assist you. When you are faced with obtaining other professional individuals' help, make sure that you are clear about what they offer and that you articulate exactly what the recipient's needs entail.

The holiday season was approaching and it would be the first Thanksgiving after Mommy's diagnosis. We came up with the idea of having Thanksgiving at her home. She was very excited and she invited a couple of her friends from the building. We decorated her place and on Thanksgiving Day, her apartment was filled with family, friends, food and laughter. It was a fun time!

As we are establishing ways to support our loved ones' physical needs we must not forget about their relational needs. We must always remember to recognize their identity, who they are and the roles they play in our lives. Yes, I am my mother's caregiver but first and foremost, I am her daughter. Yes, she is a care recipient but she is first and foremost a mother, grandmother, mother-in-law, sister, aunt, and friend.

Phase Two

Mommy's condition remained pretty stable for almost two years. During this time the original home aide had to stop working because of health reasons. That was a little challenging for a moment. Fortunately, we were blessed to have a very close friend of our family fill the position. We had established some form of normalcy. Notice I said some form of normalcy, and not a routine. Caregiving is never a routine; it can change day to day.

The phone rang around 3:30 in the afternoon. It was Mommy's friend and neighbor, Ms. Faith (this name will mean so much once I finish sharing what happened). Ms. Faith (an Angel of God) was calling to let me know that she and Mommy were talking on the phone and in the middle of the conversation she heard Mommy's voice slur a couple of times. She said she went back to talking normal and they even discussed that they both heard it. She shared exactly what I was thinking, that Mommy was possibly having a stroke. I hung up and immediately called 911 and they dispatched an ambulance. My husband and I hopped in the car; we were only fifteen minutes away but the drive seemed longer. As we drove in silence, I prayed for Mommy to be all right and I felt grateful that this happened while she was on the phone with Ms. Faith. Time is of the essence when someone has a stroke. The sooner they are able to receive medical attention the better. When we arrived, Mommy was already in the ambulance. After about 10 minutes, they proceeded to the hospital.

Once Mommy arrived at the hospital, measures were taken to stabilize her condition. After a while I was allowed to go back to her room. As I entered, I remember feeling unsure of what to expect, to my surprise, she said "hi" as I came into the room. She seemed to be alert and there was no slur in her speech. I felt some sense of relief. The doctor came in to talk and share that Mommy had indeed suffered a stroke. He informed us that some tests had been run and there would be more to come in order to determine the extent of changes it may have caused her body.

It wasn't very long at all before Mommy was transferred to a hospital room. Once she was settled in bed, armed with monitors, IV and other apparatuses connected to her, the nurse brought in a computer so that she could do a formal registration. As she began with her questions, I remember she looked directly at me when she asked what her birth date was. I turned to my mom and posed the question to her, and she answered. I told the nurse, "She can answer," and she did a very good job. There were a few questions she needed help with. This was just another sign to me that God's hand was on her and He was in control. That night I left the hospital feeling very hopeful. Mommy's hospitalization lasted 18 days, she did her rehabilitation at the same hospital on another floor. The stroke affected the right side of her brain and therefore weakened the left side of her body. Going forward she needed a walker to help her support and steady herself while walking. After her release, she continued her therapy at home.

When Mommy came home, there were definitely some adjustments that needed to be made to her environment in order for her to function comfortably. In addition to her walker, a motorized chair was ordered. Her home aide's hours were adjusted so that she could come out five days a week instead of three. Prior to her stroke Mom would prepare a few foods for herself; now she was not able to do that. I visited more frequently and prepared meals as well. Mommy always enjoyed the daily activities that were offered in her community and she continued to participate.

In the beginning things seemed to be moving along smoothly, after a few months, things started to change. Mommy's emotional, mental and physical energy seemed to vary day by day. Although meals were available to her, she was not eating properly, she had mood swings, she showed more signs of confusion and she did not always welcome the help and assistance that was offered to her. I even received a phone call from the property manager of her building expressing some concerns about her behavior around the community. As these changes began to occur, I began to consider what could be done as a solution.

As I mentioned earlier, a caregiver's responsibilities can change overnight! The decision was made that Mommy would move in with us. The expected scenario was that we would be there to provide for her needs and that she would be there for us as well. My thought was that us being together as a family unit would be a great environment for us all to thrive in.

Phase Three

Our household included me, my husband, and two daughters (ages 17 and eight). Although we all knew things would be a little different, we were excited about being together. We actually had lived together before, so we all felt it was doable.

This was a very exciting and busy time for our family. My oldest daughter was in her senior year of high school, so we were involved in that whole process of graduation and the events associated with it, as well as preparing for her going off to college. At the time I was also enrolled in a college program. We all were away from home the better part of the day. Mommy's home aide continued to come and assist her during the day. She was able to go out with her sometimes during the day and other times with us as a family, or she and I would go out as well. She kept in touch with friends from the senior community as well as other friends and family. I would even take her back to her old building on Friday evenings to play cards with her friends.

After a few months, things seemed to change. Mommy became irritable, accusatory, and had moments when she would lash out. Most of the time these actions were directed toward me. I remember thinking, *What the heck is going on?* I received phone calls from a couple of her friends as well as a few family members asking me what was going on with Mommy and me? Most were calling because they were concerned and wanted to encourage me but there is always that one, that one that you least expect, who was not encouraging and had the audacity to jump on the accusatory band wagon and was very hurtful and disappointing.

In the midst of everything going on during this season, this was a lot to comprehend. Nevertheless, I needed to address it. I called and scheduled an appointment with her physician. I wrote down what I wanted to share with him, as well as questions that I had for him. The day of the appointment will forever be embedded in my brain. Mommy didn't want to go. She proclaimed, "Nothing is wrong with me. I do not need to go to see the doctor." Needless to say, it took a lot of persuasion. Once there, we checked in, after a few minutes we went back to the room to be seen by the doctor. I shared my concerns as clearly and discreetly as I could. He briefly examined her and asked her why she was there and what was going on. She responded, "I don't know why I'm here. I feel fine. They wanted me to come here!" He then asked her the day, the year, and who was the president. She answered all correctly, and that was the end of the visit. I was done. This was a total waste of time!

Needless to say, after that, he was no longer her doctor. I began to make inquiries and do some research to find a new doctor for Mommy. I specifically wanted someone who worked with people experiencing memory loss related to dementia and Alzheimer's disease. A female doctor was highly recommended to me by a cousin of mine. She specialized in geriatrics and memory disorders related to the elderly. She also had written a book based on caring for her mother, who had Alzheimer's disease. She was an expert and that was exactly what we needed. I scheduled an appointment; it was about a month out but this divine connection gave me hope! Appointment day came and all went smoothly as far as us getting there. Mommy was very comfortable meeting with the doctor and was very receptive to her. There was consultation, testing, evaluation, and a new medication was also prescribed. She also shared vital information with me regarding the different levels of caregiving as well as resources that are available for caregivers and care recipients. Mommy was under her care for more than a year. It ended because the doctor retired.

Mommy became a lot calmer but she still had days when she was very irritated and anxious. One of the things that she continued to share when she went through these moments was that she wanted her own place. I began to think about that a lot. I prayed for guidance and direction from God because that statement began to stick out in my mind. I have to be honest, at first, I was a little hurt and offended by it. I thought that I was doing the right thing bringing her to live with us to take care of her. Why would she want to be alone? It also caused me to reflect upon what the doctor had shared about there being different levels of caregiving and the resources available. As I continued to pray about this, I was able to receive revelation that my mother still had a lot to offer others; she still was able to be a blessing to other people. Wow, this really blessed me, because she did, and I did not want to be responsible for her not being able to do just that.

I started to look into Assisted Living Facilities. There were a few facilities in the vicinity of our home. I think I contacted four altogether. I began talking to my mother about them. She was interested and wanted to go to visit. I planned to visit two of the four. When I contacted the facilities, one had no availability and the other one had immediate availability. We scheduled an appointment for a tour. The facility was well kept, they offered several activities, three meals a day along with snacks, medication distribution, in-house therapy and doctor's appointments, hair salon, outings, Bible study, worship service and other amenities. The apartments were a comfortable size and they did not have stoves in them. It seemed to be a good fit; it met several of the requirements I felt were needed to support a safe and livable environment for Mommy. During the tour I even saw someone that I knew that was working there. (More on this later.) After some discussion between Mommy and me, we decided that she would move in. Mommy moved into the apartment that we viewed because it was on the second floor and close to the elevator. We preferred this location in the building.

Mommy was excited about having her own place. I supported her enthusiasm but I still wondered if it was the right thing to do. Remember the person I saw while touring? Well, we both went to the same church. This person turned out to be the facility's Food Service Director. I actually ran into them at worship and I asked if they had positions available. I had recently obtained a culinary degree. There was an opening. I interviewed and got the job. Three weeks after my mom moved into the facility, I became an employee there. You are probably thinking, *What?* Don't judge me! I have to admit in the beginning it was a plus to be able to really see how things operated in the community and to see how Mommy was adjusting to the transition. I actually worked in this position for two years before moving on. Mommy lived in this community for a little over three years. After that time, Mommy moved to a newly built facility that was still in the vicinity of where I lived.

In addition to assessing the care recipient's level of need we should assess their current abilities. As a caregiver we must allow them to operate at a level of independence that fits their abilities. Taking over everything and not assessing the things they may still be able to do takes away from who they are and how they show up in life as well as contributing to them possibly feeling angry, sad, useless, and unfulfilled. We want them to operate at a level of thriving and not surviving. Mommy lived in the assisted living environment for over five years. I really believe that this experience allowed her to thrive as a person. She operated at a level of responsibility, independence and socialization that she was able to handle. I am sure it contributed to her self-confidence, self-worth and longevity.

Phase Four

I received a phone call around 6:00 am from a nurse at the community where Mommy was living. He called to inform me that she had been taken to the hospital because she had fallen sometime during the night. He was actually the one who heard her calling for help, went into her apartment and found her lying on the bathroom floor. I then called the hospital to find out more information.

I spoke to the doctor on duty in the emergency room and he gave me an update of her condition. Vitals were good, she didn't have a stroke, no broken bones; there was just a lot of weakness in her left leg. I went to the hospital as soon as I got dressed. Seeing her in person did make me feel better. She was alert but she just kept saying, "I don't know what happened; I was just going to the bathroom." After several days in the hospital, she was transferred to a Rehab Facility.

At the Rehab, Mommy participated in three types of therapy: physical, behavioral and occupational. In the beginning of her stay she was progressing well. She was able to stand up and get out of the wheelchair using her walker and take a few steps forward. My first grandchild was born prematurely a couple of months before Mommy's stroke and while she was in rehab, I always used her being able to see her great-granddaughter and spend time with her as a way to encourage her to participate in therapy and get better. After a while it seemed that she had reached a "plateau." Plateau is not a term you want to hear when you are in this type of environment because it usually leads to a patient being discharged. After a three-month stay, Mommy was discharged. Because of her current physical condition, she was unable to return to the Assisted Living Community because she no longer met certain requirements needed to be able to live there. Mommy was only able to take a few steps. She was not able to maneuver the wheelchair enough to get around an apartment and she was not able to do a lot of the things that she did on her own before the fall.

Here we were again, at a crossroads. What would be the next step for me as a caregiver and for her as the recipient? At this point we seemed to have only two options: Would she go to a long-term care facility or would she come to live with us? I visited several long-term care facilities before making a decision. When I visited the places, I would always have the thought in the back of my mind that my mother was not ready for this. I felt that she had so much life left in her and this type of environment would not be a good fit at this time. We decided that she would come to live with us.

Once we reached a decision, we made preparations for her arrival. The living room and dining room area of our home became her living quarters. All the necessary equipment and rearrangements to the area were made prior to her arrival. Mommy continued therapy at home. She gained strength and is now able to transfer safely with little help, which is definitely a plus because it eliminates a lot of lifting her up. Having her here has been an adjustment for everyone. After three months and several candidates I was able to get a very reliable home health aide to assist during the week. Caring for Mommy is a joint effort but I carry most of the responsibility. It has been a little over three years now. Although it has not been easy, I don't regret the decision to bring her to live with us. I have been especially grateful for that decision during this past year of the COVID 19 pandemic. I really do not know what I would have done had I not been able to visit with my mom, on my own terms. During this time, I have not solicited any outside help. We have done everything ourselves. It has been difficult at times, and everyone has had to deal with the added challenges of this horrible pandemic but by the grace of God we have made it through!

As I pen this chapter a recent memory stands out in my mind. As we brought in this new year of 2021, I remember saying Happy New Year to my Mommy and her response was "Happy New Year, Happy You Year; this is going to be your year and, in a few months, I will be 91 years old." I responded, "I receive that, Mommy, and yes, you will be 91 in June. You will see 91." I remember feeling grateful that my mother had great expectations for both our futures and she was able to articulate them. Moments like this fuel me and let me know that we made the right decision. In less than thirty days we will celebrate her 91st birthday!

Jonquia J. Vaulx has always desired to train, teach, and push people into destiny. She is a multi-business entrepreneur and the author of "There is No Such Thing As Coincidences". She is a registered Radiologic Technologist of 19 years and was an ultrasound professor for seven years, before the pandemic. She married her soul mate, James W. Vaulx, 18 years ago and they have three beautiful children; which are her heartbeat and legacy!

Jonquia started her journey to entrepreneurship over eleven years ago with the support of her husband. She started this path in the shadow of her mother, Marilyn Hall, as she taught school and encouraged everyone they encountered. She owns three businesses. Two daycares, including kindergarten; Train Up A Child Learning Centers and Orange Leaf Frozen yogurt.

She has been featured in Voyage LA magazine in December 2020, as the magazine was featuring Hidden Gems in the Community. She was a speaker for The Worthy Empowerment Tour all over the world in 2019. She is a Spiritual Leader in Northwest Indiana, volunteering on the Go, outreach team and intercessory team. She is an ordained Minister of seven years.

Jonquia is CEO of Destiny Divas and loves speaking life and positive energy into the atmosphere! She is a wife, mother, caregiver, entrepreneur and philanthropist. She is passionate about helping and serving people.

She is an encourager, and shares wisdom and life experiences to support others in discovering purpose.

DIVINE INSTRUCTIONS

Jonquia Vaulx

> *I know, O Lord, that a man's life is not his own,*
> *it is not for man to direct his steps.*
> Jeremiah 10:23, NIV

I decided to put my daughter Jayla Jewel in basketball. She loves to shoot hoops. We went to practice one afternoon and my other children wanted to watch her play so we sat together supporting our star. Jayla got hit in the head with a basketball and struggled to play.

However, her head was hurting so her coach picked her up and sat her on an elevated bleacher seat. This seat was immediately below the track in the gymnasium. I needed to check on my Jayla. She was physically hurt from the game. As she was struggling with physical pain, her mommy was struggling with mental and emotional pain. I was emotionally hurt from a debate with my husband.

Marriage is a covenant, a tailor-made union of two hearts, minds, souls, and lives. Two people becoming one in spirit is the constant, consistent goal of marriage. Genesis 2:18, KJV says, "And the Lord God said, it is not good that the man should be alone, I will make him an help meet for him." Nevertheless, that is indeed the scripture so why I felt defeated as a wife was a mystery to me.

I was seriously upset with my husband of nine years at the time of my daughter's basketball practice. I had decided I had absolutely nothing to say to him. The morning of practice we had debated all night. I was tired and fatigued in my spirit, not to mention feeling stubborn and irritable. I was having a flesh moment. "For the desires of the flesh are against the Spirit, and the desires of the Spirit are against the flesh, for these are opposed to each other, to keep you from doing the things you want to do." Galatians 5:17, ESV

I decided to go talk to my daughter to see how she was feeling after being hit in the head with a ball. As I sat in the gym, I could hear the spirit of the Lord say, "Go to the track upstairs." On my journey upstairs, not knowing how to get to the track, there was a room with a glass wall, appearing to be a dance or aerobics class. I know my Father's voice and I could hear, "Go in there." I opened the door; the room was empty. I looked on a table by the door and there lay a book.

The title of the book was *The Power of a Praying Wife*. The title astounded me. I got the message from God loud and clear! The flesh moment must come to an end! I need to PRAY for my marriage! Galatians 5:16 states, "But I say, walk and live in the Holy Spirit (responsive to and controlled and guided by the Spirit); then you will certainly not gratify the cravings and desires of the flesh of human nature without God." God is so awesome! He went a step further. I looked in the inside the book—it was MY BOOK! My name was in it, with notes I wrote and telephone numbers I had written. AMAZING…

"Cast your bread upon the waters, for you will find it after many days." (Ecclesiastes 11:1, ESV) I gave the book to someone—I don't even recall who—approximately three years ago. The book surfaced right when I needed it most.

As I went to check on MY daughter, God was giving divine instructions and checking on HIS daughter!

As time passed in our marriage, trouble did not completely pass over. Trials and tribulations are a part of the path of development. We hit another roadblock in 2016. I was ready to leave my church home—the place we grew together, got baptized together, developed relationships with spiritual parents together, and had babies christened before the congregation together. Well, I felt I was not valued on the ministry staff and it was time for me to go, without the agreement of my husband. My husband would say, "Pray, be quiet, and be still!" He said, "Peter sank because he took his eyes off of Jesus." My response was, "I am telling you there is a witch in this church and she is being embraced!" My husband replied, "I did not say the wind and waves were not real on the stormy sea; I said stay focused on Jesus!" Well, I felt the leadership was not listening, and my husband was not listening or giving me the response my flesh desired. At this point, I decided I would "do life" only with our children. I even told James, my husband, "YOU can stay here."

Rebellion had set up in my heart. I would come late, leave early, and look at social media when I attended. I began visiting other churches ALONE. I knew it was not the order and timing of God because I felt like I was out of order. The reason I say out of order is because you can do right the wrong way. I had no peace with leaving the church at this time and a person should never leave a church, job, marriage, or any relationship if God has not given divine instructions.

I could not understand, while in the midst of this season, if God confirmed what He told and showed, why there was so much chaos in MY life. I was the help meet to my hubby and the right hand to my First Lady. In my perspective I was on point. After months passed, God was clear to inform me, "Everything I show you is not to be repeated, communicated, or fought for." The Bible says stand still and see the salvation of the Lord (Exodus 14:13). It's not our job to go against our covenant partners in warfare.

In Genesis 9:21-29 Noah drank of wine and was drunk. He was uncovered; his son Ham saw his nakedness inside the tent. He told his two brothers. Shem and Japeth took a garment, and laid it upon him as they went backward, covering his nakedness. This is important because when nakedness is revealed in people—vulnerability, flaws, hidden agendas, and ulterior motives—we must pray. As growing Christians, we can take on a spirit of self-righteousness or a spirit of control with the "right" intention, which is not pleasing to God. We cannot hide behind the word Christian and think we have it all together. As the Apostle Paul said, we are forever learning. Wisdom is the principal thing. A bridled tongue can solve problems and not add gasoline to a lit charcoal grill. We should speak life using wisdom in every conversation. I expressed to several intercessors what God showed me, and that can turn to gossip quick. We are to shut up and pray. We are called to cover our husbands, wives, pastors, children, families, and enemies. When we cover, and not converse, we dispel darkness.

The wisdom from my husband was to be quiet and pray. If I had listened my heart would not have hardened and I would not have been going religiously to multiple churches, with undirected steps. I almost forfeited my assignment in my church as a minister. The drama in my marriage was at a climax. My divided house was headed to divorce. I even tried to pick up my book, *The Power of a Praying Wife*, but I had no desire to read it or pray anymore.

Matthew 12:25 states, "…every city or house divided against itself shall not stand." Remember when you desire to do good evil is ever present. In the words of my mother, "It's not what you do, but how." As I did not listen to the wise counsel of my hubby, my flesh was caught up and ALL could have ended in disaster. The Bible says, "There is a way that seemeth right, unto man, but the end thereof are the ways of death." (Proverbs 14:12, KJV)

In due time, just like Judas, the "witch" eventually exposed and hung herself. I graciously was restored for cutting her ear off, like Peter.

I practically derailed destiny in the area of unity in marriage, integrity of my position in the local church, and my heart toxicity.

In the words of my current Pastor in 2021, "Witches need deliverance too." If they keep showing up and the Holy Ghost-filled are in correct prayer posture, all we encounter can be transformed. Prayer breaks chains, renews minds, and purifies hearts. Prayers of the righteous availeth much. God does not put a stop sign up and say she, he, or that situation is too dark or complicated for breakthrough. We are to be wise as serpents and gentle as doves.

We are to watch as well as pray.

I have been with my spouse 24 years and married 19 years. God continues to get the glory! I decided to allow God to truly be the head of our covenant and me. The choice is ours. "Yet amid all these things we are more than conquerors and gain a surpassing victory through Him Who loved us" (Romans 8:37). Psalms 37:23, KJV states the steps of a good man are ordered by the Lord, and delighted in His way. I have learned to sit still with God.

Flesh moves can leave your destiny, ministry, and marriage in an incubator. I stand proud of my growth, courage to trust, and accomplishment of learning submission. Submission does not mean to shut up and sit down when told. It means to trust your husband to lead, protect, and provide. The question I pose to my readers is, what do you do when you feel like you are walking in a season alone? You have been faithful, been in your prayer closet, received answers and it seems everybody around you is asleep! Three scenarios: asleep and in denial, aware and unresponsive, aware and judgmentally angry. Jesus told His disciples, "When I needed you most, you were sleeping" in the garden of Gethsemane right before the most difficult moment that would be the final step to complete his assignment. This was before His crucifixion and His inner circle went to sleep. I am convinced it is in the darkest seasons we have to walk only with GOD. Sometimes, it feels as He is absent. He lets us finish our process and then the puzzle, the sacrifice begins to makes sense. So I say to the child being molested: I believe you. God will heal you. I say to the friend who always gives and others are condescending and not a "friend" to you: God will send the right circle. I say to the employee and church member who goes over and beyond, you feel invisible and ignored…God sees you. I say to the wife and mother, if nobody says thank you…God appreciates you. In every scenario I pray God will direct your steps to the right people at the right times in your life. Growth and stretching hurt. Romans 8:28 tells us, all things work together for the good of those who love the Lord and are called according to his purpose.

Today, I pray and keep my ears open to hear divine instructions and wisdom from God and my husband. God gave his only begotten Son, Jesus, that we all may be saved. He desires repentance for his children. He desires we live abundantly for HIM. We are one body with many members. If the toe gets infected we should attempt to treat it and not cut it off with no attempt at restoration. The cut-off culture is real in 2021, so before we judge and abandon, let us be STILL, be WISE, be INTENTIONAL, be TALKATIVE to God, be CHALLENGING in love to the spirits we encounter, be the HANDS of God and bring light to darkness. S.W.I.T.C.H. the witch. This acronym means turn on the light (switch) in darkness.

I operate using supernatural divine instructions by being the light!

Dr. Aronda Howard, PhD, MSW, LCSW

Dr. Aronda Howard's passion for children and meeting the needs of the underserved, has led her to devote over 25 years to social work administration with foster care youth and displaced populations; quality assurance, and policy analysis. For the past 12 years, she has also been teaching a variety of social work courses as an adjunct professor.

Dr. Aronda holds a Bachelor of Science in Social Science, Master of Social Work, and Doctor of Philosophy in Social Work.

Dr. Aronda is the mother of two adult sons, and Umi to her three grandchildren. For relaxation, she enjoys participating in family activities, reading, connecting with friends, and relaxing at the beach.

James 1:12 – Blessed is the man who remains steadfast under trial, for when he has stood the test, he will receive the crown of life, which God has promised to those who love him.

MOST IMPORTANTLY, I'M A DAUGHTER OF THE KING

Dr. Aronda Howard

A Daughter who had three fathers here on earth;
A Daughter who became emotionally disconnected from her mother;
A Daughter who was a teenage mother;
A Daughter who is an overcomer of domestic violence in an abusive marriage;
A Daughter who became a mother of sons;
A Daughter who became an Umi to her grandchildren;
A Daughter who became a Social Worker;
A Daughter who became an Advocate for the abused and unprotected;
A Daughter who became a College Professor;
A Daughter who became a Prayer warrior;
A Daughter who became a sister to many—Sister/Sista/Soror;
A Daughter who became a Woman who holds a Bachelor of Science in Social Science;
A Daughter who became a Woman who holds a Master of Social Work Degree;
A Daughter who became a Woman who holds a PhD in Social Work—

From beginning to Everlasting, I'm a DAUGHTER of the KING of GLORY, the KING Strong and Mighty!

Growing up, from my earliest memories, I felt loved by two men, both of whom I knew as my father—one whose last name I carry, and one who carried me in his heart. I carry them both in mine. My life experiences with each of my fathers, my mother, my family, siblings and extended family has left an indelible print on my heart that has reverberated throughout my life. While the independent experiences with my parents were not inherently malicious, it was hard for me, a little girl coming of age in a complex world, to navigate the complexities of those relationships. My relationship with both fathers was strong, but nevertheless, part of an exacerbation of the psychosocial crisis of adolescence and the struggle in the formation of my identity. From my earliest memories of childhood through the dissolution of my marriage, I felt like I was always chasing a sense of belonging to someone.

I have five older siblings with whom I was raised, who all had the same mother and father. I have carried their father's last name most of life. Carrying his name for me, at times, has been a source of frustration, conflict and pain. He was married to my mom, but he knew he was not my father. He accepted me as his child. Their dad—our dad—DAD, as we call him—always made me feel loved when he was around. At the time of my birth, however, DAD was not around. During my early childhood, I also felt loved/supported by Dad's family, especially by Dad's brother, me and my siblings' favorite uncle, who doted on all of us and made me feel like I was everything. One Thanksgiving at my siblings' paternal grandparents' house, someone asked why I was always there. I think I was about eight years old. That was my last Thanksgiving there. It was the beginning of fully knowing what I somehow already knew. I didn't belong there. These weren't my grandparents. This wasn't my real family. I had a family out there somewhere.

Around the age of 12, I found out that Dad, the one whose last name I carry, was not my biological father, but rather another man—the conduit—a man from whom I had been completely estranged, or so I thought. I remember going out to dinner with my mom and godmother and having them tell "the truth" about my father's identity. They assured me I had seen him many times. He worked at a hospital about three blocks from where our family had previously lived. It was the hospital where my siblings and I received all of our well child care, and apparently, he watched me play on the playground a lot when I was a much younger child. He and my mom were childhood friends. He reportedly kept up with the details of my life. I was so confused. The migraines started. My biological father, the conduit, was a mystery to me. From all accounts, he was smart, funny, witty, loving, and educated. Yet I knew no intimate details of his life. I didn't know his favorite foods, colors, likes, dislikes, or habits. Everything I knew about him was surface level. This thrust me into a whirlwind of unknowing and questioning: Who am I? Am I worthy? Why all this? And why isn't he interested in really knowing me?

I began seeking. I wanted to know my "new" family—cousins, aunts, grandparents, siblings—yet the conduit was disinterested in facilitating the reunion. It made things complicated, more painful. His unwillingness to engage added more questions than answers.

I spent portions of each holiday, some birthdays, special occasions, graduations and other memorable events with my biological paternal relatives. My paternal family did their best to welcome me in. I loved getting to know them, developing relationships with them and coming to love them. My aunts so were funny; they kept us all laughing. Learning the famous desserts my grandfather made and all about my grandmother's church and community engagement was exciting. My cousins and I were all attending high school at the same time, in the same city. Three of us graduated from high school on the same day. It was beautiful that my grandmother made it a priority to be there for all of us, running from one graduation to the other. My cousins and I had lots to talk about. We could go out together. We were growing up together, in a way. It was refreshing to finally be able to look in the faces of people who look like me: same build, similar features, mannerisms, quirks. I became a middle child—no longer the baby—now a big sister with a baby sister and big brother. Unfortunately, the conduit was often missing from those family events to help me make sense of it all. On a rare occasion, when I was about 16, he and I had a chance for an in-depth discussion. He said he hadn't been around because I didn't need him. My mom was married and I had a father. He felt it was best to leave well-enough alone; I wasn't the child he needed to worry about.

At first, I externalized the pain. I became angry and rebellious. I ran away from home.

Then I internalized the pain. The migraines persisted. IT was too much. I was so HURT and CONFUSED. I deserved better. I needed an explanation that made sense.

But I kept seeking GOD. I kept going to church. I kept praying. I stayed on the Usher Board. I sang in the Youth Choir. I participated in church-wide activities. I was sure I had pain written all over my demeanor. I felt weird inside. I was certain all of the adults in the youth groups, choir, and Usher Board could see it. Yet no one reached out to me. My pain was either invisible or ignored.

Perhaps this is where I began to compartmentalize pain to protect others. Perhaps this is where I learned to put on a good face.

My Pops, my father of the heart, was hurt too. It was as if he didn't understand why any of this mattered—why was I visiting with my birth father? He and my mom met when I was a year old. I became his baby girl, and we had been inseparable ever since. Here he was still standing TALL since day one, being MY everyday HERO: all birthdays, school days, summer vacations, school plays, Saturday mornings eating oysters at Lexington Market, family car rides, proms, award ceremonies, graduations, teaching me to how to love out loud, how to live life, making every holiday in my memory happen. My Pops met every daily need as provider-protector-priest of his household, and he did it in love, no strings attached. He thought his baby girl was pursuing the love of another man—the conduit. That wasn't it at all. Yes, I wanted my biological father to love me, fully acknowledge me, show some interest, but mostly I was just trying to get clear. I was trying to figure out who I was. It was so much for me to carry. It seemed NO ONE understood. NO ONE was happy with me. I felt like it was all my fault. After all, no one talked to me about it.

It was as if after I was informed that the conduit was my father, somehow, I was to reconcile all the pieces of my brokenness without any additional information. What could I do? Who could I talk to? I CLUNG to GOD and I queried Him. I kept going to church. Prayer became my constant companion. I needed a mentor too. But I didn't know where to get one. So I prayed. I petitioned God. I waited for the download. I kept moving.

In those early days during late adolescence, I clung to a relationship with my oldest son's father and his family. I became a mom at

19, a pivotal point in my development, at which time I still needed active parenting. Kept pushing. Couldn't look back.

I became known by my attributes— over-achiever, churched, dependable, even good mother—the outward expression of self. I was much loved. My family has often spoken proudly of me. I was everyone's baby. My mama's youngest child. My maternal grand-mother's youngest grandchild. My godmother's baby girl. The family's baby girl couldn't possibly have any legitimate problems.

I excelled at my education. I PERSISTED. Bachelor's degree. Kept going. Master's degree. Kept going. Doctor of Philosophy. Ok. Goal achieved. Always holding on to my hope that my emotional pain was not going to do me in. Luke 1:37—"For Nothing will be impossible with God"— became one of my favorite scriptures and daily mantras. My reminder to keep pushing.

I CHASED GOD all over Baltimore, going from church to church. I wanted the pain to stop and I thought that for me the balm was in the church. At some point it crystallized that while I loved the fellowship, God was within me always. Then I began to breathe and allow my pieces to come back together.

During this period of inner turmoil and growth, I learned:

God designed me, and therefore I am His daughter and my identity is in Him. 2 Corinthians 6:18, NIV says "And I will be a father to you, and you shall be sons and daughters to me, says the Lord Almighty." Therefore, when I couldn't get the answers I needed to questions I didn't ask, I developed my identity in Christ. I allowed the WORD to become flesh in my life. I became His daughter and not just a member of the church. I trusted God's plan for my life, no matter what obstacles appeared, and I kept my hope in the LORD above things.

God's power is all-encompassing. Yet it is in our weakness that He makes us strong. 2 Corinthians 12:9, NASB reminds us that He has said, "My grace is sufficient for you, for power is perfected in weakness. Most gladly, therefore, I will rather boast about my weaknesses, so that the power of Christ may dwell in me." When we surrender to Him, we see the glory of His of Power revealed in us. If we just keep the faith, be strong and courageous, we are reminded that God is with us and He will always be a strong tower for His daughters. God is passionate about the work He wants to do though each of us. He will bring us through experiences that help us hear and feel the heart of His people.

Through this experience, I developed a deep sense of passion for the needs of children, particularly the well-being of children who have been abused and neglected, with a window into the hearts and minds of girls. While I don't see my personal adolescent experience as abuse or neglect, I do see it as a missed opportunity for intervention by the systems with which I was already engaged—the family, the community, the school, and the church. Through my personal experience, my life's work evolved. My passion has shown through my career path as well as how I extended myself in various households of faith. I've been able to channel my relationship with Christ, and the deep abiding love that I feel as His Daughter into how I love my children, how I work with children and families in my professional work, and how I engage with girls and women in church and the community.

Colossians 3:14, ESV reminds us, "And above all these put on love, which binds everything together in perfect harmony." Therefore, when I reflect on my adolescence, LOVE still wins. In the midst of my pain, God reaffirmed Himself as my Father, and me as His daughter. He never left me. I've always felt God's incredible LOVE for me as I worked through my pain.

There were many roads I could have traveled. Many things that I did that during my adolescence could have taken me far away from God, as I processed my hurt, but HIS abiding LOVE for me always drew me back to the altar, and to the Throne of Grace. Out of a deep hurt and longing for an unhindered earthly father, the seeds were planted to meet the needs of unwanted children – abused, neglected, mishandled, misunderstood, misguided, unloved, and unprotected both here and abroad.

I used the experience as a catalyst to help propel me to further my education and help me learn to help others. I became a professional social worker and I have spent more than 25 years working in the Child Welfare System. I believe my lived experiences helped to develop my compassion for children who experience adverse experiences of childhood, and specifically a window in the minds and souls of girls and women.

During this particular experience, God was pruning me. At times, I was very frightened, but I was constantly aware of God's presence. And I was constantly aware that He was preparing me for greater, that He wanted more for me and from me and that He gives power to those whom He can trust. I now know, I had to allow my flesh to die and hold on to His Grace. And in the process, remember to keep a cheerful heart. The work He was preparing me to do—both within the Kingdom and World—would require me to decrease and allow His Glory to increase in all things. It began with me trusting Him during the turbulence of my adolescence, so I could allow Him to work through me in the area of Child Welfare and Adolescent Development.

Isaiah 40:31 happens to be one of my favorite scriptures. It's a reminder of God's power, a reminder to keep moving, to keep trusting God to continue to renew you on your journey.

I learned to pray without ceasing. To petition GOD. And to have an expectation of answered prayer.

I also began studying the Bible for myself and included self-help instruments too.

> *"Identification with an organization or a cause*
> *is no substitute for self-realization."*
> *– Swami Rudra Nanda*

My childhood and adolescent experiences propelled me to develop a heart for the lived experiences of children and youth. My lived experience also created turbulence, which exacerbated the typical psychosocial crisis of adolescence and spilled over into my early adult life. Through my experiences, I developed a heart for the mitigation of poor psychosocial outcomes related to primary, secondary and tertiary experiences of childhood. The stabilizing factor for me was my FAITH. The CHURCH was a safe haven for me, but there were many missed opportunities for the church to minister to me. God was always with me, but I needed the women in the church to be more active. As a young girl, I needed to be evangelized and mentored. I needed to have someone impart the WORD to me on my level, deliberately. I also needed someone to step out and have courageous conversations with me to help me make good decisions. I felt compelled to share my story to help the church consider ways to prepare in anticipation for the tumultuous time of adolescence in the lives of girls; to develop an operational stance that life is going to happen, and the effects of life can be far reaching, unless timely and appropriate interventions are readily available.

Girls are at risk in our communities. Often we think of risk as the big-ticket items—girls seemingly "running wild," juvenile delinquency, child abuse, promiscuity, etc. However, family discord, changes in family dynamics, changes in family functioning, and poor communication are often the precipitating factors in the psychosocial crises of adolescence.

> *"When you can look a thing dead in the eye, acknowledge that it exists, call it exactly what it is, and decide what role it will play in your life, then, my Beloved, you have taken the first step toward your freedom."*
> *– Iyanla Vanzant*

Four Action Steps We Can Take within the Church to Mitigate the Effects of Family Conflict for Girls in the Church, and Confirm GOD's Purpose, Power and Passion for His Daughters:

1. Listen to Their Stories
   a. Create safe places for girls to express themselves and share their lived experiences
   b. Have guided/facilitated discussion
   c. Don't wait for signs of trouble; expect adolescence to be a period of trouble

2. Acknowledge Their Journey
   a. Be willing to have courageous conversations
   b. Validate their experiences even when we do not understand it
   c. Stay knowledgeable about current trends in adolescent well-being

3. Connect Girls to Appropriate Resources
   a. Have a ready list of relevant resources
      i. Free
      ii. Online
      iii. Community-based
      iv. Grounded in sound biblical teaching
      v. Grounded in adolescent well-being (Biological/ Psychological/Emotional/Social/ Educational/Trauma Informed)

4. Teach Girls that they are Daughters of the King of Glory!
   a. Girls need a foundational identity in Christ
   b. Make it ceremonial for them

Bonita McFadden is the founder of Elevation Consulting Services. She is a financial specialist helping families create generational wealth plans. She understands that everyone is unique and has a purpose, thus creating the Defining Womanhood group. It is a safe place for women to come and discover purpose as they heal from trauma.

Her unique journey to recovery has been painful at times, experiencing death, divorce, illness and homelessness. But it has taught her to value each day. She believes everyone has value, and that she also should be valued.

Bonita wants to open a recovery center for women to learn how to live out their purpose, by starting with loving themselves first. She is a product of the wonderful healing power and grace of God. Bonita has four amazing adult children and two awesome granddaughters that fill her world with joy.

Bonita believes life is worth living so live it to the fullest.

YOU ARE UNIQUE
Bonita McFadden

Unique is defined as existing as the only, or as the sole example; single, solitary in type or characteristics; incomparable. (dictionary.com)

Growing up this word was used often when my family would describe me. I grew up in a time when light-skinned black girls with long hair were all the rage. I was the opposite. My skin was caramel and my hair was short. For the most part, I was a happy child. I was raised by a single mom who made mistakes along the way (Who didn't?) but wanted the best for us. I was the oldest of two. Even though we looked like a normal family on the outside, inside the four walls of our home, it could be challenging. I was trained to stand up straight and make eye contact with people. I was taught to be kind to everyone, no matter their background. This at times got me in trouble. I was known for fighting for people who were being picked on. I grew up in Englewood, which is on the south side of Chicago. It was a middle-class neighborhood where everyone knew each other. At times this was challenging because everyone on the block had the right to correct you, whether that was with words or a belt. I was raised to say "yes ma'am" and "no sir." Which is all great. It taught me to respect my elders. I loved growing up in my neighborhood.

My mom always wanted better for us. At Christmas time we would drive to Evanston and look at the mansion decorations and dream it was our house. "Nothing is impossible with hard work and God," my mom would say. For special occasions, we would go to an expensive restaurant. It showed me a life outside of my local community and I was grateful. But it would take me years to learn how to manage my emotions, how to manage disappointment, heartbreak, and loneliness. I had to learn how to "just get over it"—words no child at any age should hear. I first heard these words after my grandfather died. He was pulling the water hose in and he fell. I was a few days away from being twelve. I watched him fall and later that night he died. I cried for weeks, maybe even months. I was told to just get over it. You have to get better. But how?

I grew up in a traditional Baptist church setting. I was in church from sunup to sundown every Sunday. It was in this setting my training to be a leader began. We had countless groups to participate in. It was in church I began to discover different abilities. It was natural for me to speak well among my friends and small groups. It was not natural to speak or sing in front of large groups. It was like a spotlight was on me all the time. I would become sick to my stomach or I would freeze up. This continued throughout high school too. But like most children, I just wanted to fix it. I didn't want to stand out in the crowd. Even though at times I did. So I quickly learned to do "just enough" in school and life to fit in. As a teenager, I discovered that my personality was larger than life at times. I remember entering high school and yet again being made to feel inadequate because I didn't have long hair or light skin. So I joined a group of "mischief" girls who didn't care about my looks. I was introduced to drugs through these ladies. It helped to ease the pain of life. This feeling of wanting to belong tormented me for years. But deep inside I knew that I was different from most people. When I shopped, I would buy unique pieces. I never wanted to be dress like anyone else. I'm still like that today. There's something about having something that belongs only to you.

But back to my journey: In high school, I had several difficult experiences that led me into survival mode. The first was the loss of the family business. My family owned and operated a soul food restaurant. The store attached to ours burned and the gas build-up exploded into our restaurant. This was unimaginable at the time. My family went from having financial security to having to deal with limited resources. My life was changed forever in a moment. I watched my grandmother go from being someone who helped everyone to having to constantly ask for help. At times it was embarrassing. It felt like we were begging all the time. I watched my mother accepting a manager position at McDonald's and later at a bank to make ends meet. She was miserable. I saw the light in her become dimmer with each experience of life. We experienced electricity, phone, and gas services being shut off. It happened during a time of uncertainty in my life. I was a junior in high school and everything I thought was secure was not. What could we do now? These words led me to a life of struggles to get back to a place of financial security.

I was hurting and no one noticed it. I realize that was because they were hurting too. I was alone and scared and no one knew how to help. I had a plan for my life and it was turned upside down. The friends I thought would be there for me were not. I entered a place of seeking approval and love from all the wrong people. God gave me a big heart to love. With my upbringing, I was taught to trust and be kind. But I had to learn how to love in a way that honored everyone in the relationship. Unfortunately, this process led to me hurting some people and being wounded myself.

The next thing was, at seventeen, I became pregnant. I thought we would get married and live happily ever after. Well, it was the opposite. He was the first boy I had ever been with and he denied he was the father. I was devastated. I had my life planned out. I was going to graduate from college, then get a good job. I was going to be rich by 30. It was all changed with one decision. I went from hopeful to depressed. How did this happen? I was supposed to do great things. This led to finding unhealthy ways to medicate the pain. Sex, drugs, and alcohol became my pain relief.

The loss of important people in my life seemed endless. But the greatest of these was a childhood friend. She had it all together. She was beautiful, confident and kind. Our conversations were everything to me. She was older and I respected her opinion. For the first time in my life, I felt accepted for me. She didn't judge me based on my looks. She was the first person to see the beauty in me from the inside out. She would encourage me to do my makeup (never really wore it) and dress to impress every day, no matter what. Her friendship was everything. I never thought it would end. But she fell in love and her soon-to-be husband didn't like me. So our friendship ended and it took years for me to recover. I felt rejected. I didn't understand then but I do now. So I fell into the drug scene deeper and found fake friendships that devastated me even more. I just wanted to belong. I wanted to feel important and valuable. I wanted a real relationship again, whether that was romantic or friendship. This led to one bad romantic relationship after another. My life was falling apart and I didn't know to fix it. How was I even going to get out of this mess I created? I fell into depression and began isolating myself.

During this time, I had three more children. I love my children. They are amazing individuals. Being a single mother and young was challenging. I wanted the best for every one of them. I wanted their lives to be filled with joy and especially love. I wanted to give them their hearts' desires. Unfortunately, there were times I couldn't and it broke my heart. I thank God for a loving family who helped care for my children when I was missing for days on drugs. Words can never express my gratitude for their help, especially my sister, who has always been there for me and my children. She has sacrificed in ways I cannot explain. So how to do you change a messed up life?

My grandmother was a praying woman. During that time, it didn't make sense to pray. God was mad at me for all the right reasons. My life at this point was out of control. I deserved everything that was happening to me. But thanks be to God, that's not the way he operates. I thank God for a praying grandmother and mother. With my life spiraling out of control, it was their prayers that changed my life. On July 3, 1995, I walked out of the crack house into the church house and never looked back. My journey to recovery has taken many twists and turns. The first step was embracing my past choices and decisions. This was a series of steps to forgiveness, the first being myself. I'm still forgiving myself daily. I had to forgive myself for making bad decisions. I had to forgive myself for not completing assignments in a timely manner. I had to forgive myself for not being a good mother. I had to forgive myself for not being a good friend. The biggest of these is forgiving myself for not being uniquely me. Next, I had to ask for forgiveness from my family. This was difficult because I had put them through a lot. Even though they forgave me, it took a long time to trust that the change I made was real.

Let me encourage someone. Don't allow anyone's decision to guide your change. They don't dictate your outcome. You do.

During every fear, doubt, and uncertainty I have learned to trust the process God has for me. I'm fearfully and wonderfully made (Psalms 139:14). I am unique. On this journey of recovery, my scripture has been Jeremiah 29:11: "I know what I'm doing. I have it planned out—plans to take care of you, not abandon you, plans to give you the future you hope for" (The Message version). This has been comforting to me over the last twenty years. By no means have I been perfect but his new mercies daily continue to guide my decisions. It gives me comfort and peace. I wake up each day grateful for an opportunity to get it right and forgiving myself if I don't. I pursue better choices and make a difference, which is my choice too. I love on purpose and forgive those who don't understand me, those who misuse me, those who talk about me wrongfully. I embrace each new day as a gift. I know my story might sound like others but it's not; it's my story. I am who I am today because I was able to embrace my story. I no longer care about what people think or feel about me. I am delivered.

We are only granted one life and I plan to live the rest of it without limits. So I challenge every little girl to pursue her dreams, no matter how outrageous they may seem to others. I challenge every twenty-something to become focused on a goal of greatness. I challenge every thirty-something to thrive and not settle. I challenge every forty-something to arise and live on purpose. Finally, my fifty and beyond friends, we are not too old to fulfill the dreams we once had in our twenties. Arise and shine so that our legacy will be great in the land. I AM Unique!

Can anything good come out of Mississippi? Yes indeed! Her name is Sharon Weatherspoon. Sharon has a bachelor's degree in Business Administration from Delta State University and a Bachelor of Religious Studies from All Saints Bible College.

Sharon Weatherspoon is the owner and founder of Lead2Edify, LLC. She is a certified John Maxwell leadership coach/speaker, a Destiny Training Academy life coach/mentor, a published author, and a prophetic, revelatory teacher with a pastoral grace. She has served in ministry for over 25 years in various leadership positions.

Sharon's life's motto is "Just do what God says." Although Sharon experienced many childhood traumas, she has been beautifully healed and made whole by God's overwhelming love. God has given Sharon an assignment to restore women, teaching them how to receive His unfailing love and the blessed gift of purity and wholeness. She is and will always be a well-loved woman who is #UnapologeticallyVirtuous.

LOVE-DRIVEN
OUT OF THE SPOTLIGHT
INTO OBSCURITY

Sharon Weatherspoon

She was the quiet one. Her books were her friends. A peculiar child was she and so content to sit in her bedroom and just read for hours. It was not only her daily escape, but it was her dream time. She spent most of her time in her bedroom and little with her siblings because she didn't seem to click with them. Sometimes she wondered if she was in the wrong family because she didn't quite fit in. She wasn't like any of her siblings. The fact that she looked so much like her mother chased away the silly notion that maybe she was adopted. She wasn't the baby of the family, but she was treated as such, which caused much retaliation from her siblings. When she read that story in the Bible about Joseph's brothers putting him in that pit and then selling him, she finally had someone she could identify with. You would think that this was enough childhood trauma for one little girl, but there would be more challenges that she would face. It started during the summer before going to the 7th grade. Although nothing could compare to her books, she thought she would try out for the basketball team because she had the height. On the first day of practice, she was injured, leading to a doctor's visit. The doctor's visit led to the discovery that she had cancer. And just like that, she missed her entire 7th grade school year. This little girl was blessed with two loving parents, and their love for her carried her through one of the greatest battles that she would ever have to fight. Cancer ravaged her fragile little body, and it fought hard. Cancer lost the battle, and the experience would ultimately lead her to a life-changing encounter with Jesus. Jesus won her innocent little heart.

Ok, why am I talking about myself in the third person like John did when he wrote the book of John in the Bible? Maybe it's because I'm still in awe that I actually was that little girl, and I'm still amazed that many didn't survive, but I am still here by the grace of God, and I now live at the pleasure of the King of kings.

My momma had nine children, and I'm number eight, the knee baby. At an early age, I was a wise child. I watched my momma whipping my older siblings, and I took note. Therefore, I dodged a lot of whippings. It wasn't that I was such a good child, but I was scared into being good for fear of the switch. You know, the ones you had to go pull off the tree in the yard that was used for chastisement. Well, because I didn't get very many whippings, my momma declared me to be her good child—the one who never gave her much trouble. I was the child who cried when my siblings got a whipping, so of course, I was going to do everything I could to be "good." I was unaware that this wanting to be good to please my momma would manifest in a harmful way in my adult life.

It's funny how being a "good" person grew to become the spirit of rejection. Symptoms of this spirit of rejection in my life were perfection, insecurity, and pride.

As I stated above, I had childhood cancer. It was a horrific experience, but I survived it. I didn't finish my chemo treatment. It was doing me more harm than good; therefore, the doctors stopped the treatment, but God healed me. During the time I was on chemo, I was angry with God. I had stopped attending church. I felt upset that God would allow this to happen to me. A couple of years after I was in remission, a friend from high school invited me to her church revival. I don't know why but I accepted the invitation. Back then, they did five nights of revival. I was convicted that first night and should have gone to the altar and gotten saved, but I was too scared. I went every night, and on that Friday night, the last night of the revival, I made up in my mind that I was going to surrender my life to Jesus, regardless of who else went to the altar. Something in me changed that night. I grew up going to church, but that night I had a personal encounter with the Lord. My relationship with Jesus got sweeter every day. One night while alone in my bedroom, I was talking to Jesus. I was thinking about all those children who had died that had the exact cancer I had and had taken the same chemo treatment that I had taken. Many died, but God allowed me to live. That night I asked Jesus if He would let me bless as many people as possible before leaving this world. It was my way of just wanting to thank Him for giving me life.

I was unaware that my upbringing to be a good child and my desire to be a blessing would cause the seed of performance-driven to manifest in my life. It was the absence of balance in my life that caused the manifestation. Both things together or alone are good and desirable, but they can be harmful if not correctly stewarded. I like Haagen-Dazs ice cream. It is good, but too much of it will add pounds I don't want and possibly harm my general health.

I was not familiar with the culture of the church I joined. I grew up a Methodist, but this was a Pentecostal Church. I was hidden in plain sight in the church during my high school and college years because I didn't know my gifts and calling. After graduating from college, I asked God to give me a good job where I had my nights and weekends free because I wanted to be faithful to attending church. I wanted to know my gifts and calling. My Pastor at that time prayed and fasted with a group of us who were seeking our calling. I did whatever my hands found to do. I did start to notice that when I was called upon to teach Sunday School, the Holy Spirit would fall on me, and I could teach with revelation. No longer hidden, my gifts began to grow, and I became sought out. It seemed most everyone in my local denomination knew my name. One seems to get noticed when you can exercise your gifts. A noticed gift leads to pressure to "perform," which ultimately leads to burnout or depletion. I learned from my spiritual burnout you must pour out of your abundance and be poured into just as much or more as you pour out. I discovered that it's best to never minister from an empty place. It's like letting the gas tank indicator drop to E, and now you're just driving on gas fumes, praying to make it to the gas station before the vehicle stops.

Let me pause here and give you Webster's dictionary meaning of performance.

Performance is a public presentation or exhibition, the manner of reacting to stimuli.

Oxford American Dictionary's meaning of performance *is the capabilities of a machine, vehicle, or product, especially when observed under particular conditions.*

I shared these definitions because I don't want us to see performance-driven as a negative connotation. Performance is a good thing. Successful people are performance-driven. It's when there is no balance in how we perform that it can be harmful. Now here is my definition of performance-driven. For me, it was when my desire to be a blessing connected with people's need to be blessed by the gifts and calling on my life. When I ministered, people's expectations pulled on the gifts in me, and I gave my all every time. God was so merciful that when I was ministering on empty, He still blessed the people.

I learned from this experience that you always need an inner circle of people who can pour into you once you've poured out. Replenishment is necessary! Let me say that again. REPLENISHMENT IS NECESSARY!

I want to share a little of Elijah's story with you. It's recorded in 1 Kings 18:19-46 KJV, and 1 Kings 19:1-21 KJV. God greatly used Elijah. He stood before the prophets of Baal and declared that God was the one true living God. It was an epic battle. Each group had to build their altar but could not use fire to light it. The god of each group had to supply the fire. The prophets of Baal failed miserably. They cried and even cut themselves, but their god was a no-show. Next, it was Elijah's turn. Not only did he build an altar, but he poured water all over it. Not once, but he poured water over the altar three times. Elijah called out to God, and the fire of the Lord fell from heaven and consumed the burnt sacrifice. Elijah won the battle, and God showed Himself strong and mighty. Right after this incredible display of God's power, Jezebel sends Elijah a threatening letter, and he goes into hiding. Why would a man who had seen such a move of God be running from a threatening letter? I believe the answer is in 1 Kings 19:14 KJV:

And he said, I have been very jealous for the Lord God of hosts: because the children of Israel have forsaken thy covenant, thrown down thine altars, and slain thy prophets with the sword; and I, even I only, am left; and they seek my life, to take it away.

Elijah felt that he was alone. He did not have an inner circle to encourage him and pour back into him when he had poured out so much on Mount Carmel. Notice what God did in 1 Kings 19. God sent Elisha to minister to Elijah. Elisha told Elijah, "Where you go, I'm going with you."

I was like Elijah. I had many people around me who admired my gifts, but I didn't have an Elisha in my life. It led to spiritual fatigue and burnout. I was seemingly thriving on the outside but so spiritually tired on the inside. Everyone knew my name, but nobody felt my pain. During this time, I frequently fasted for spiritual strength. I was 105 lbs. My doctors repeatedly told me that it was unhealthy for me to fast the way I did, but I refused to listen because I was trying to get spiritually full. God had given me the assignment to go to church and pray. He didn't give me any instructions as to how many days or the length of time. I guess I should have asked for further instructions. I would go to church and pray every evening after I got off work. I shut in on Friday nights and some Saturday nights because I wanted more spiritual strength. Yes, I was a godly woman, but my life was way out of balance. The excessive spiritual discipline of fasting and praying was my compensation for not having an inner circle to pour into me.

I just wanted to be a "good" and faithful servant just as I was a "good" daughter to my momma. God demonstrated His power so mightily through me. I literally saw God work many miracles.

The only thing that shut me down was my mother's death. God had shown me her death in a dream, but I prayed and prayed that it would not be so. I grieved for a long time, but I kept doing the work of the Lord. God in His mercy told me to surrender my Missionary Evangelist license and leave. I didn't obey Him immediately. One reason was fear, and the other was shame because EVERYONE KNEW MY NAME. It took some years for me to obey God. It was one of the hardest things that I have ever had to. I entered a winter/wilderness season. It was winter because one day I was doing all this work for the Lord, then very quickly I wasn't doing not much at all. It was a wilderness because God just told me to leave. He didn't say where to, and I didn't know where I was going. The next few years, God began to restore me and make me whole in a barren wilderness season.

I loved the landscape at my previous place of residence. There was a beautiful bunch of yellow flowers (my favorite color). I never found out what kind of flowers they were. They bloomed so pretty, but during the winter season, they would die out to nothing. The ground was barren. I didn't realize that these beautiful yellow flowers would be in full bloom again at the appointed time.

I was in my barren winter, wondering what had I done to make God put me in a time out, but He knew that I needed rest, and I needed to stop pouring long enough to get full again. The days turned into weeks. The weeks turned into months, and the months turned into a few years. God was restoring my identity in Christ. He was pouring out His love on me.

I remember one particular day when I was sitting on the sofa. I felt His presence and, in my spirit, I heard Him say, "Sharon, if you never do anything else for me, I still love you." His words brought me to tears; they broke something off of me. He loved me for me.

That night I began to go on a love journey with the Lord. I was an outcast, ashamed, and in hiding, but in this season, I was getting to know the love of God extraordinarily. I had always loved God and knew that He loved me, but this was a more profound, intimate experience. These two scriptures below were illuminated in my heart and became my daily meditation.

> *That Christ may dwell in your hearts by faith; that ye, being rooted and grounded in love, may be able to comprehend with all saints what is the breadth, and length, and depth, and height; and to know the love of Christ, which passeth knowledge, that you might be filled with all the fulness of God.*
> *Ephesians 3:17-19, KJV*

> *I know that you delight to set your truth deep in my spirit. So come into the hidden places of my heart and teach me wisdom. Purify my conscience! Make this leper clean again! Wash me in your love until I am pure in heart.*
> *Psalm 51: 6-7, TPT*

The Lord, in His great love for me, drove me out of the spotlight into obscurity. I didn't realize how spiritually tired I was and how much I needed to rest and receive the love of God. I can remember driving to work, and when I got to a traffic light, I would open my arms and stretch them out wide and say, "Father God, I open wide my heart to receive all of the love you have for me today. Fill me with the fullness of your love. Get in every nook and crevice of my heart." I would feel His presence wash over me, and the tears would flow. I didn't know that there was so much healing just by receiving the love of God.

This barren season was like that beautiful yellow flower. Just as that flower shed its beautiful blooms, I had to spiritually box up all the tremendous accolades and trophies I had received. I had to clear my spiritual mantel to have nothing to compare to what God was getting ready to do in me! As Isaiah 43:19 KJV says, "Behold, I will do a new thing," and I don't even want to hinder God by the knowledge of what He has already done in me! I was far away from where everyone knew my name, a place where I was celebrated. His great love was driving me out of the familiar and into the place called destiny.

I was growing in obscurity in a hidden place. Father God began to restore my identity in Christ Jesus. He was reminding me that I was his beloved daughter, chosen for good works. I was starting to bloom again. I was becoming the Sharon that Jesus' love built. My desire to be a blessing was reignited. But this time, the source of my passion was His love for me. I didn't want to bless others just to be doing something good. I now wanted to bless others from the depth of His love for me. As a well-loved woman, I can wholeheartedly say that I no longer live a performance-driven life. I live a love-driven life!

Arise (from spiritual depression to a new life), shine (be radiant with the glory and brilliance of the Lord); for your light has come, And the glory and brilliance of the Lord has risen upon you.
Isaiah 60:1, AMP

Love-Driven

All my life, I've been driven by something. Driven to be good because momma said I should. Driven by fear of how people see me because of the residue of what cancer took me through. Driven to perform in my gifts by my desire. Driven to reciprocate my thanks to God for reversing the devil's fate for me. But now, I'm finally driven by the overwhelming love of God. I didn't realize the length and the depth of His amazing love until I was at Sharon's end. It was at that place He took my shattered heart and supernaturally made it over again. Now my heart can carry God's overflowing love that will never end. And everything I do from this point to eternity is only because His love is driving me.

Shatiki Beatty is a mother to four daughters and one grand-daughter. She has a passion to assist people in discovering their strength through sharing her life's experiences and strong faith. Although losing the school board election, her Schenectady County Human Rights individuals' rights nomination was recognized for her advocacy in equal access and accountability in health, education, and quality social programs, working with Ellis Medicine, Schenectady Chapter City Mission, and Bridges Out of Poverty.

Shatiki's ability to connect with many walks of life provided her with a healthcare consultant coaching position with Schenectady City Mission. She was promoted to assist in program development of Empower Health, a grassroots healthcare program addressing health and social determinates of health for people or families in crisis. Their success grew to provide some with full-time employment. Through street level engagement and telephonic strategies, patient health compliance improved, and reduced emergency department utilization; winning a competitive New York State $300k healthcare grant expansion.

RESILIENCE IN HARD TIMES

Shatiki Beatty

Often times we throw ourselves into our work for personal satisfaction because we haven't defined what happiness looks like within.

Where's your happiness? Is it within your title, like mine: mother? Do you push yourself so hard to be the best that you forget who you are? Can you sit with yourself and be at peace with the decisions you've made for you and your family? If not, come with me. Let's unpack. As you will see, you must become okay with your decisions, when you are in authority to make them. Your power, your voice, is waiting to make a stand. What does your self-care look like? Who's in your corner? What's their purpose? Are they on your side? For months I struggled, trying to make sense of who this person was. I had no idea that I was a woman because I was rejected as a woman. Because my most intimate relationship, of a mother and daughter, was traumatically severed. It would take a global pandemic, fighting to cover my family, and healing from God to know I was healed. The best decision I made in my life was letting go and allowing God to heal me. My healing made me face my greatest fear and gave me courage to set boundaries and always operate in love.

Certainly, if my biological mother were alive, she would be so very proud of me. I feel her presence with me every day. Being a mother was something I always wanted. Being separated from her at a young age was the beginning of the hardest trauma that I would ever face. It also served as my foundation to keep my family safe. As the second oldest of her five children, I took responsibility for the trauma we endured. I could not keep us safe and now we had to separate. I was fortunate to be with my oldest brother; however, my heart yearned for my younger siblings. I worried about them. We had a hard life. I would always make my daughters' sibling relationships a priority. It would take many years of psychotic medication, episodes, substance abuse and therapy sessions to know how deeply my heart hurt from not having the loving support of and everyone's God-given right to a mother's love.

Many years later, for some reason, I understand her. I understand why she would decide to give her five children into a corrupt New York state foster care system rather than let her family raise us. I connected with her decision the moment in my motherhood where I felt I would rather walk away from my children than not be my very best for them. Our most intimate and precious protected relationship begins between a mother and her child. When this relationship is interrupted, both of these people will always emotionally look for or pull toward those relationships typically found between a mother and child. There's safety in that relationship and as an orphaned child this perceived abandonment meant I struggled with relationships, bonding relationships, because of deep severed intimate relationships, such as with my mother and siblings. This leads to unhealthy boundaries, and some relationships end.

I am a sinner. I birthed three daughters from a married man and thought my forever karma was chaos. Unfortunately, I made a commitment to motherhood long ago that my daughters would know their siblings, which meant having a relationship with them. This relationship meant they would spend time together outside normal court hours because it meant that much to them as well. There was a price to pay. Unwanted and unannounced visits to my home became the norm until enough was enough. Don't let people manipulate your good intentions. Your values are important and need to be held respectfully. Keeping unhealthy boundaries leads to chaos.

I feared losing my daughters. Losing my children was my greatest fear. It was a large part of why I became intentional about what I thought the ideal mother would be. I was determined to connect with people I admired, who would teach me how to shed and build. Not everyone signs up to be on your team. We tend to invest so much of ourselves into others, including our dreams, that we become disconnected. The things that I strove to do were in honor of my commitment to be a great mother.

When the Lord began to work with me concerning loss, He focused on relationships, which took me to the relationship with my biological mother. I asked, "What about that relationship?" Relationships require intimacy, because intimacy is connection; the need to belong – to connect with someone who cares about you. You can be a surrogate parent. The mother is still connected to the child, intimately, although they have no relationship. This explained why I loved people the way that they are. Our connection. Like the relationship with Colliens and I. We met when I first became a mother. He stopped by to help me decorate for my daughter's birthday party. He was so amazing with my daughter. He became her godfather. We were a little family. I called him dad. I also referred to him as my gay husband, as he was out loud, vibrant and lovingly gay. He absolutely loved God with every fiber of his being. I loved that about him. He lived his life to the fullest. As a young woman, I needed him to be there for me. He was my strength and my safety but sometimes the help felt like competition and I wanted no part of that friction. You have to be watchful that the people surrounding or influencing you are doing so to help your vision, not because you're their competition.

Throughout the years, he would stay with me to help as my family grew. I am so thankful to God for our memories and our family. It was one of the sweetest relationships I've had. We disagreed at times concerning my daughters because I allowed him to always have a voice, often greater than my own. There is a ten-year gap from my youngest to oldest daughter and times had changed as we did. I began to hold onto my daughters tighter because I didn't want our house divided. There were times when he and I did not talk because of it. It would hurt so badly. I did not know how to include him in my decision making when his investment was temporary. I did not want him to take over; however, his personality allowed it.

We have to stop taking from people just because it is offered. Helpers have to welcome independence since it should be the ultimate goal. Co-dependency is an unequal debt.

I would miss him; however, the Lord is kind and He revealed that power and authority are different. Shortly before his untimely death, he thanked me for treating him like a man and allowing him to feel a part of a family. It meant so much to know he understood, but I just wanted to know one thing. Was I a good mom? I asked him if he understood why I had to let go and hold on. He cried so hard and said he could not have done better himself. I was left for dead so many times, most times through my own self-destructive responses. I told him the Lord is kind. He told me that I'd be strong when it was time. I felt like I lost my mother again. Yet I had to push aside what I was feeling to be a good mother.

We all face those dilemmas because we are all pouring from one place: mother, sister, employee, neighbor, nephew, etc. We remove a little anxiety off the top to make it to the next day when deep down, we did not have the strength to get up. We have so many things happening at once that we have not taken the time to unpack the moment. Unpacking moments is a term I referred to during my counseling sessions. I discovered that you must empty out events and not push them aside. Simply because something makes intellectual sense does not mean that you are not hurting. For example, you may understand the negative behaviors of an addict, but that does not mean someone stealing from me does not hurt. I always stop at intellect because emotions are very intimate and true to me. I am very sensitive and instantly connect with someone's energy.

I got up and showed up for my daughters. Every day. When they rebelled against me, I felt betrayed and angry, at first. I felt I had created a life for them to be successful. I did not understand when we became disconnected. When I got advice that it was normal, I could not accept that rebellion had to be a normal part of adolescence. It felt like I was at war. I didn't want to give up but I did not know what else to do. I didn't think I did enough for me until the Lord said I was enough.

Sometimes we keep trying to improve a relationship when we should be celebrating. I had accomplished so much, yet none of it was enough because what I needed, I'd lost. I wanted a relationship with my daughters like I always dreamed of. I could not understand how to separate my dream of being a good mother and how it could not be as valuable as a dream for a career or a car. How could I let this go? The Lord was kind to let me understand that my intimate relationships were damaged. I was hurting, and losing him opened up some pain I was too afraid to feel. Well, the problem was me. I was so focused on my motherhood and all its beautiful character that I forgot about me—a beautiful black woman who needed to be respected. I forgot I was enough. I had spent so much time improving as a mother, daughter, sister, etc. that I was hurting my most intimate relationship; my relationship with myself. I started with *no*. It continued with *I'm ok with you being upset with me*. Then it continued to *I'm still loved even if you no longer want me*. I found out that I was ok.

The more you enjoy you, the less time you want to spend with people who don't value you. Anywhere. I protect my peace at all costs, with no exceptions. My boundaries are necessary and I'm deliberate about maintaining them, which means certain behaviors were not tolerated. I needed to release people from my expectations.

People will try to use your vision against you. The Lord is kind to let me understand that people must serve your weakness to release you from the weight of it. I don't argue with anyone determined to misunderstand me. I make their choice my decision. Before long, you will begin to enjoy life on life's terms. Don't be held hostage to your past or to the expectations of other people. You are free to create whatever world fits for you and your family. Guard your heart and protect your peace. You're not going to have all of the answers right away. It is ok. You are enough.

Queen GerVaise Sarah Guyton is a Powerhouse global speaker, award winning Best-Selling author, CEO and Co-Founder of Forever Guyton Publishing, LLC, a sex-abuse and domestic violence survivor.

GerVaise provides an environment of healing when she speaks, providing hope and insight that inspires survivors and the non-abused alike to seek healing and wholeness. Through her #1 Best-Selling book The Dirty Man: A Memoir of Healing and Deliverance from Sexual Abuse, now available on Amazon; she transparently shares her real, raw, and unapologetic journey to restoration, elevation, and wholeness after experiencing years of sexual childhood trauma and domestic violence as an adult.

THE ELEVATION OF A QUEEN DURING LOVE AND WAR

GerVaise Guyton

What a difference sixteen years makes! Sitting in the waiting room awaiting the arrival of the first addition to our family, April 9, 2005, changed my life forever. A new love was birthed that day, capturing a piece of my heart for infinity. Looking into his eyes helped me realize how much I desired and valued the love of family. His birth marked the breaking of a generational curse in our family bloodline, where a two-parent household was not the norm. I grew up in a one-parent household that operated from a void where love and acceptance should have been. Their brokenness cultivated a household that led to five years of sexual abuse from their lover, The Dirty Man.

After fleeing an abusive spouse, my custodial parent ran to the safety of a local church, where the pastor became my godfather, the most consistent male figure in my life, becoming my sex slave master in my teens. The consistent love bombing and withdrawals created a crumbled foundation littered with sharp glass pebbles and random material, like the abandoned empty lots on the south side of Chicago. Learning that love had to be earned by deeds and unrealistic sacrifices became the standard and expectations of those who said they loved me.

The Dirty Man is a multi-millionaire who became our human form of GOD and savior for my family and others within our community. The longing to have a solid family and living in a state of peace and fulfilment seemed like an impossible dream. Despite knowing the family I was introduced to from my earlier years, the ability to freely go and visit was not allowed. We could not miss any services nor leave early from church. My grandfather was 65 years old when I was born so he was already in his later years from my birth. He was a wealthy businessman, and he did not like the consistent control The Dirty Man had over my sibling and me.

I remember at an early age, he and my custodial parent arguing about how ridiculous it was for us to be on the bus in the brutal Chicago cold, wearing dresses because he made the decision we could no longer wear pants. Despite the religious organization not allowing women to wear pants we always wore them, until new church mothers joined The Dirty Man's church. I vividly recall him yelling at my parents, saying, "You are a fool! Having those girls outside in waist-high snow in long skirts and dresses while his kids are warm in a car—what sense does that make, Jay?" One year my parent became upset because Grandfather decided to buy my sibling and me snowsuits with pants, and this was one of the last snow gears he purchased in my adolescent years.

The truth is, my grandfather demonstrated the love, correction, and support that could have made the absence of my non-custodial parent moot but The Dirty Man and my custodial parent continued to minimize his ability to be that person. This makes perfect sense why I felt trapped, alone, afraid, and helpless when the grooming for sexual abuse started at the age of 14. We were only allowed to stay over at our grandparent's house after church on Friday night and had to be back Sunday morning. We could not go to my Grandma Lucy's church; it was required that we returned to The Dirty Man's church. This was not by coincidence. The Dirty Disgusting Man, the Satanic Ruler (DDM SR) needed the most vigilant male in my family to be seen as a threat and unloving so he could maintain complete control over my mind, body, and soul.

My custodial parent fostered an environment of catering to every ludicrous request, even requesting I give my virginity to The Dirty Man because of all he had done for my family, literally crying tears and begging me to allow this dirty old man to rape and molest me on-demand under the explanation of "LOVE" and support, often using what I have learned to be grooming and reverse psychology on my family. At times we would be in The Dirty Man's church office, feet away from the pulpit and altar, and he would have me walking around naked while others were in the holy temple of GOD. The closed thin wooden door was the only thing that concealed the sexual abuse from unknowing church members.

Often, he called me from playing and trying to have a social life with fellow teens who attended this cult called a church, requiring me to perform oral sex, raping me on the couch, recliner, secretary's chair, desk, and his black office chair, which was nestled behind his large desk. After each sexual assault he would clean" me up by getting a warm washcloth from his in-suite full bathroom. At times after service, there would be leading members of The Dirty Man's office present and I would be instructed to give him a massage from his neck down to his feet.

As an adult reflecting on such moments, I asked the question why did not one adult confront him in those moments? If a married man summoned a child to massage him while in my presence, there would be a confrontation, followed by a report to the authorities. No one questioned the multi-millionaire whose wife was home with their younger two children—the blind eye and unspoken acceptance created by a culture of dismissing apparent signs of abuse for convenience and accepting the status quo. **My first jewel** is to say something if we see a sign of possible sexual abuse. Become informed with the key language and signs a victim may demonstrate. One in 10 children is sexually abused, and 90% of them know their abuser. Eliminate and reduce isolated, one-on-one situations to decrease the risk for abuse. Under no circumstances should an adult male be rubbed down with an office full of adults or left alone with a concealed door with no opening for anyone to see inside at any given moment. It was never my job to protect myself as an adolescent or teenager; as adults we must take responsibility for the child(ren).

The conflict for me was the acceptance and coaching. My biological parent gave full access for him to have his way with me on demand. No, my parent was not a drug addict or alcoholic; their addiction was love and the desire for acceptance. For years it was a struggle to grasp the why and how on my parent's part. It is an age-old dysfunction that, if left unaddressed, can have a generational impact, which was one of the reasons they agreed and did not see anything wrong with their choices at the time. I remember being awakened by my biological parent to make sure I was showered and clean for The Dirty Man to have his way with me. The ritualistic cleaning before bedtime was not to keep my sheet clean; it was to make sure my body was ready to be violated. The Dirty Man never physically chastised me with a belt; he would use the rape to keep me in line, often saying what I better not do anymore while his member violated every orifice of my body.

The fact is, my parent was just another tool at his disposal. I recollect receiving a call from my custodial parent's cell phone. They were screaming and begging the Chicago Police Officer to take them back to Illinois since they did not want to have sex with the Police Officer. The conversation lasted what seemed like an eternity. He kept saying, "No, let us go up NOW! I bought you dinner for your birthday; now let us go to the room." The parent kept saying, "No, take me home. I want to go home!" Frightened, worried, and feeling helpless, I clicked over to call The Dirty Man since the Chicago Police Officer was his close friend. He said, "Oh, they will be just fine," then hung up. My determination to save my parent did not stop there. I three-way called 911, the local Chicago Police station, my boyfriend Big Jay, and a family friend until the phone went dead. The Dirty Man had permitted the Chicago Police Officer to have his way with my parent.

After calling and seeking answers The Dirty Man came and picked me and my sibling up and we slept in the church. The next day before the car wash opened the Chicago Police Officer dropped my parent off with their hair, which was freshly curled the night before, all over their head. Fear and a gripping reality set in after this horrific experience. My parent could not save themselves; how in the world could they save me? **The second jewel**: No one, including a parent, can give beyond their ability and acceptance. If a person chooses to be delusional to help themselves cope with their own agenda or desires, no words can force them to change a second before they decide it is time. No love, sexual gratification, cooking, cleaning, friendliness, law-breaking, ride or die loyalty, granting every desire of their heart at the sacrifice of one's own will ever convince them. It is an independent walk of truth promoted by a spiritual influence that brings clarity and change. No, this reality is not a free pass to have others step all over a loved one's needs or neglect one's own boundaries. It is important to establish boundaries early on and maintain them. I share the specifics of being physically abused and ultimately the freedom journey from The Dirty Man in my award-winning, best-selling debut book *The Dirty Man: A Memoir of Healing and Deliverance from Sex Abuse*. The physical removal from both my custodial parent and The Dirty Man did not heal me instantly.

The residual impact of the five years of sex abuse, and the many years of grooming before the onset of the sexual abuse created a huge rift in my family relationships. Despite two additional family members living through similar sex abuse experiences by The Dirty Man, the trauma did not bring us together. While in the custodial care of my parent it was always ingrained in me to look out for my sibling, while my sibling was taught to watch out and report back to them anything I would do. At times, my sibling would take gifts, to keep them quiet, from my boyfriend who wanted to talk on the phone or go to the movie while on punishment. After taking the gifts they would then tell The Dirty Man and my custodial parent, resulting in more trouble for me. It was the best of both worlds and the good child award for them. My strength to act was heavily rooted in my perceived failure to protect my sibling, who was also victimized from the age of 12 until we departed on July 4, 2001.

The legacy of my grandfather, to see our family love and support each other lives on in my desire as well as other family members who recognize the value in doing so. God sent an amazing King, Ronald H. Guyton, Jr. You can learn about his significant contribution to my life in *The Dirty Man* in the chapter titled "Oh, the

JOY!" It outlines how he fostered a healthy home environment for intense healing, emotional support, and the blueprint for who my little king aspires to be. The latter was cut short since our family lost our king suddenly, when our son was only three months old. About a year ago my friend Kim W. said, "When I learned what happened, the first thing I thought was, she just had her baby and now her husband is gone." I broke down in tears because she really understood me and knew my heart. Her understanding freed me in a way I had not experienced until that moment. My love for family and sisterhood has been a challenging ebb and flow since my siblings have not reciprocated this level of loyalty and consistent love.

I am number nine of ten biological siblings on my father's side. As of the time this chapter is written, only one brother, Dan T. Sr., and his household have reached out to congratulate me. It has been over a month since my book reached the best-seller status, along with other awards, and the sibling I have been closest to has not acknowledged or congratulated me. That has not been my example set and maintained since our physical freedom and it once deflated my plans and dreams because of the lack of blood support from a sibling who knows some of the pain firsthand. How does one love a person despite their toxic traits? I use the success of REST principles – Restoration and Elevation of a Survivor's Trust, the healthy healing place. To learn the details of how to REST visit my website: QueenGerVaise.com/REST. My healing did not automatically transfer to my sibling.

In fact, in November 2018, while heading to vote, I stopped by my sibling's home to deliver some items for my nephew. I heard God clearly: "Call to let them know you are en route." That was odd since I had full access and normally did not do so. Upon speaking they informed me they would let my nephew know to meet me outside, which was also odd. When I arrived The Dirty Woman, who was a toxic spiritual parent who maliciously used me spiritually, financially, and continued to reap the calculated benefits of my siblings and I taxing relationship, which carried over from our years of sexual abuse, was there. The sibling continued the spiritual connection with The Dirty Woman, despite knowing the financial abuse and manipulation used to take advantage of my real estate property, which The Dirty Woman justified doing for the sake of advancing the "kingdom" of God and the embassy. When my nephew came to acquire the things, The Dirty Woman began to yell my name, "GerVaise come here, you not gon' speak?" I politely waved and continued to speak to my nephew, providing instructions. The Dirty Woman continued to demand I get out of the car to speak to her. I continued to sit in the car communicating with my nephew. She yelled yet again and pointed to the ground as if I were a dog, shouting, "Come here GerVaise!"

I respectfully said no, waved and proceeded to back out of my sibling's driveway, pointing to my wrist, saying I had to go vote and pick up my husband. After confirming the delivery my sibling called me asking what happened at their home. I explained what happened and they proceeded to say I disrespected their spiritual authority in front of my nephew and my leader would not accept such disrespect. My reply was that my leader had more important things to worry about than me not coming to speak to him; a wave would be equally acceptable. They proceeded to attack my husband and compare him to their spiritual authority. I informed them, a more appropriate comparison would be The Dirty Man to The Dirty Woman, since my husband was the same, but the parallels of their leadership were just like the dysfunctional, abusive, toxic environment we grew up in at The Dirty Man's church.

There is no way I could sit under a spiritual leader who manipulated over six figures out of my sibling and justified it by saying I was foolish and attacking my character. The sibling then blocked my ability to communicate with my nephews because they felt I disrespected The Dirty Woman by not getting out of the car, which violated me on so many levels. The Dirty Woman has repeatedly shared with my nephews present in the congregation my sexual intimacy with Mr. Mac, telling everyone to stay away from me, which is also outlined in *The Dirty Man* book in the chapter titled "Same Trick, Different Sex." The Prophetess conveniently left out that she connected me with Mr. Mac, saying I would marry him in months and not years.

When I left The Dirty Woman's church, I told her I could not hear her preach about character and integrity while not operating with integrity. One day my sibling expressed a sudden interest in connecting with the various sexual abuse and domestic violence charitable and not for profit organizations I had established decades of relationships with. This was a dream come true since I had suggested for many years that we heal as a team so we could help others to do the same. After hours of picking my brain, completing the screening, background, and signing up with the shelter home I referred, while leaving near the end of the months of training, my sibling yelled while pulling off from the class, "Ok, Prophetess." Utter disappointment set in; The Dirty Woman knew my lengthy history of working with shelter homes. Prophetess wanted me to be the director for an organization she wanted to start before leaving. It was crystal clear my sibling only reached out and picked my brain because The Dirty Woman put them up to it, knowing I had the plans already written.

Despite the dysfunctional relationship with my sibling, God laid it on my heart to fast and pray for their mind and children because of the negative influence The Dirty Woman had over them. After arguing with God and trying to negotiate my justified reasons for not carrying in prayer, three confirming words were received that I did not ask for, but I knew what I had to do. The love for my family has not changed. Yes, there have been a tremendous number of disappointments which required boundaries to be established. **The third jewel** is to recognize your identity and walk in it as an unapologetic Queen. Yes, I know my purpose is to share the blueprint of removing the guilt, shame, and embarrassment, helping others to be free from the torment of sexual abuse and domestic violence, demonstrating how peace, wholeness, and REST are possible, while accomplishing one's purpose and personal goals. Do you know your purpose and identity? Please take a moment and reflect on this question and implement the necessary tools for success. If you do not know where to start, let us connect and clarify your purpose.

Sharing my various forms of trauma survivorship is to demonstrate the reality that purpose can persevere even when we want to quit. Yes, I have wanted to give up at times, but the call to arise as a daughter was greater than my NO! Today, I share with you the reminder that respect and boundaries are required for friends and family members alike. The family members stood by and aided in the attempted murder of my purpose, from The Dirty Man, with my parent, to The Dirty Woman, with my sibling. The impact of both family members and spiritual leaders had lasting effects that cost me greatly. My grandfather once stated, "Everything has a cost, even if you do not know it up front." As an adult, I understand the cost must be paid. Even if a person chose to give a gift, that item cost them something, no matter how small the price: everything from an investment in time to learning the skill or trade and money. While my grandfather was explaining and teaching this lesson The Dirty Man convinced us as teens my grandfather was being selfish and out for a buck. The reality was, The Dirty Man knew if we learned that lesson his tools for manipulation and control would no longer work.

The divide and conquer was his consistent weapon of choice. When my sibling and I started our independence journey, July 4, 2001, my custodial parent continued to stay connected and worked as his personal slave at the car wash for an additional 14 years. Just as he did with my sibling and me, he had the fellow church brothers and sisters believe the poison that my parent was alone, and no one wanted to be bothered with them, concealing the fact my parent chose to stay and be with The Dirty Man instead of healing and repairing the God-given assignment of parenthood. The Dirty Man would force us to spend major holidays at his family house, denying us the ability to spend time with loved ones we wanted to make memories with—no family dinner with our own and limited time with our boyfriends when we became teens. The Dirty Man played on the divide and conquer when we left our custodial parent, telling his family members he had to have my parent there because my sibling and I did not want to be bothered with them. This was far from the truth; little did The Dirty Man know intercession and prayer were going up on my parent's behalf—not only from me but those who knew them and our story of bondage. God graced me to be a vessel of love and spiritual warfare for my parent's deliverance. In May 2014, physical deliverance took place, and my parent left The Dirty Man, the church, and the car wash as free labor. Miracles do happen, Queens, as I write this chapter there is a new freedom God will perform and that is my sibling, and their family will be delivered from The Dirty Woman.

It was challenging but a confirmation that I am a sister and daughter who has arisen! Maturity is demonstrated when we can choose love and war on our loved ones' behalf while respecting ourselves and enforcing healthy boundaries. This year my nephew I mentioned at the onset turned 16 years old. I was not invited after asking both my sibling and my nephew what the plans were. My nephew turned to his parent with a look of confusion. This was the third time in four months my son and I were not a part of his cousin's birthdays. My sibling insists it was not intentional but this was the first time it had happened since any of them were born. The adult choices of my sibling have caused my son to feel left out as an only child who's been e-learning all year with no other physical peer interaction. Prior to Christmas 2020 we had plans set in stone and two days before Christmas I was informed, via text, they were going to go visiting others instead.

My little king's paternal grandfather gave my sibling and their family Christmas greeting cards, Visa gift cards, and gifts. Around noon on Christmas Day, I informed my sibling of the gifts and they told me to come that evening since they were heading out. Upon our arrival, large cartoon balloons, cupcakes, and multiple pizza boxes were there while they cooked Christmas dinner. We were offered slices of leftover pizza. I later stumbled upon the cupcakes. The spouse and my sibling complained about how expensive the balloons were, which made it clear they hosted an event which included celebrating the youngest nephew. After I addressed how this made us feel, my sibling explained, "Someone else wanted to celebrate my nephew's upcoming birthday," failing to recognized even if that was the case, they canceled plans with my son and me to accommodate the last-minute request, which was connected with The Dirty Woman yet again.

The demand to choose The Dirty Woman over one's own healthy family relationship is their way of maintaining control. Some years prior that would have had me in a state of depression, but this time I recognized my choice to return to Illinois after being asked by my upper management to go for a management role with the largest entertainment company in the world, to ensure the birth and relationship was established with this nephew meant nothing since the tainted relationship with my sibling supersedes my role as an aunt. At times, the disappointment made me regret the level of investment, then it became clear, this is who I am: an overcoming, caring, loving, giving, and supportive Queen who had to establish and maintain boundaries since those who accepted and wanted my assistance did not have a limit. The ability to retain a level of love with boundaries has molded me into a Queen, mother, sister, and daughter who continues to Arise!

Cassandra Williams is a registered nurse and future women's health nurse practitioner. She desires to one day open up her own practice serving the adolescent community. She is passionate about her relationship with God and loves to serve others.

Cassandra has a love for reading and writing and loves to travel. She serves in her local church in whatever capacity that she is needed. She always provides a listening ear to those in need and is always willing to lend a helpful hand.

She is a giver and loves to encourage those around her to push forward and become the best that they can become.

She is passionate about leading and helping women discover their purpose and overcome obstacles that are in their way. She is breaking her silence and allowing her voice to be heard.

TRUSTING GOD AGAIN

Cassandra Williams

It was March 2016, and I had just passed the NCLEX and was now officially a registered nurse. I was beyond excited because this was a major accomplishment for me, and it was something that I had always dreamed of. Now that I had passed the boards, it was time for me to look for a job. I was always told that as a new graduate nurse it was best to work in medical surgery to gain experience, but medical surgery wasn't where my heart was. I had a passion for pediatrics/newborn and NICU, and that was where I wanted to work. I began the application process and applied at multiple hospitals for every position that would hire new grads. Initially, I had gotten callbacks and started going on interviews, but they always said that they were going with someone who had more experience.

The days started to turn into weeks and the weeks started to turn into months, and it was now summer, and I still hadn't gotten a job. Most of my colleagues that I had graduated with had already gotten jobs, and I began to get discouraged. The enemy began to place doubt in my mind that I would never find a job and that God wouldn't answer my prayers. I tried to remain hopeful as I continued to apply for different nursing jobs and continued going on interviews. My hope and faith were running low because I was starting to run out of money. I had spent all of the money in my checking account and was now into my savings. Every interview that I went on I heard the same thing: "We need someone with more experience." "We've decided to go with a more qualified candidate." I often wondered how I was supposed to get experience if no one would give me a chance.

Finally, I experienced a breakthrough. It was October and I had gotten a call from a nurse manager on an endoscopy unit. Endoscopy was something that I had no knowledge of, and it was somewhere that I didn't see myself working but I decided to give it a chance because at this point, I needed a job. I went on the interview and was hopeful. I went with an open mind and presented myself in the best way possible. The interview went well, and the manager said that she would reach out to me in the coming weeks if I had gotten the job. I was nervous, but I trusted God and believed that if this was for me, it would be for me. About two weeks later, I got a call back from the manager that she was going to hire me for the position. I was overjoyed and thanked God. Orientation would begin on December 5, and I had the month of November to get all the paperwork and everything else situated. I was grateful that someone had given me a chance.

December 5 had finally come, and it was time for me to start my first job as a registered nurse. I had all of the emotions running through me – fear, anxiety, excitement, and worry. I didn't know what to expect but I was open, willing to learn, and wanted to make a good impression. The first two weeks of orientation consisted of in-classroom training for the hospital and then after that it was more specific to the unit. After these two weeks, it was time to start on the endoscopy unit. The nurse manager paired me with a preceptor who would teach me everything that I needed to know to be successful on the endoscopy unit.

While working with my preceptor, I made sure that I paid attention to everything that she was saying, and I made sure that I asked questions if there was anything that I didn't understand. The world of endoscopy was new to me and I wanted to ensure that I was putting my best foot forward as a new nurse. I didn't want to give anyone a reason to say anything bad or negative about me, so I made sure I was on my A game at all times. As a new nurse and new employee, I knew that I was being watched at all times by everyone, so excellence was my standard. As my orientation on the endoscopy unit progressed, I became more intrigued with all things endoscopy. Although my passion was newborn/NICU, I tried to make endoscopy work and fit me. As I started the second month of orientation on the unit, everything became routine to me and I got comfortable with what I was doing. Although this was happening, I still thought that I could stay here and work. I began to research different certifications for endoscopy so that I could stay there and work my way up. This wasn't my heart's desire, but I continued to settle. My heart wasn't in it and each day at work was more a task for me than fulfillment. I would count down the hours until it was time for me to go home each day.

I talked to my mom about me staying on the endoscopy unit long-term, and she knew that wasn't what I had wanted. It was as if I was trying to convince myself that this was the place that I was sup-posed to be even though I knew that wasn't true. As I continued to work with my preceptor, she began to give me more independence on the cases that I was working on. I was doing well and becom-ing more independent and confident in what I was doing. I was learning as much as I could and doing well in retaining everything that I was learning. Then one Friday in February things took a turn for the worse as the unexpected happened. That Friday morning, I went to do some classes and training with the nurse educator. After that I was scheduled to go back to the unit after lunch to meet with my preceptor. The training went fine, and the nurse educator scheduled me for some more classes for the next week.

I went back to the unit and looked for my preceptor. I saw her as she was finishing up one of the cases in one of the rooms; she saw me and told me to wait for her in one of the rooms. I waited in the room and wondered what we were going to do for the rest of the day and what kind of cases we would see. My preceptor came in the room and closed the door and started off by saying that my manager was going to let me go. I looked at her, confused, as my stomach dropped, and tears began to form in my eyes. "I know," she said, "I'm just as confused as you are, and I don't understand why they are doing this and why now. You're progressing so well, and I don't see a reason for this." By now I was crying, and I asked her if I had messed up in any way or had done something wrong. She had said no and then said that they decided that they needed someone with more experience. She was telling me because she wanted me to know, as my manager wanted me to walk into her office blindsided. I thanked my preceptor for taking the time to teach me everything that she could as I gathered myself together before I left the room. As I walked down the hall, I saw my manager and she asked me if I could meet her in her office.

As I sat in her office and waited for her and the clinical coordinator to arrive, all I could feel was anger brewing inside me. I was hurt. My manager came in and began to speak and commended me for doing such a great job thus far. She then followed up by saying that although I was doing a great job, they had decided to let me go because they needed someone with more experience in the area and wanted someone who could move through the orientation process quicker. I just stared at them blindly as they spoke.

My manager continued to say that she hired me because she saw on my resume that we had attended the same college and grew up in the same neighborhood and that she saw herself in me and wanted to give me a chance. She then concluded by saying that if I needed anything that I could always reach out to her, and she gave me her phone number. Trying to hold back tears, I remained as professional as possible and thanked her and made my way to my locker. I felt so hurt, used, and taken advantage of.

I got to the hospital lobby and through tears called my mom and told her what happened. She was just as shocked and in disbelief as I was. She was upset and she couldn't believe it. I made my way home and cried that whole weekend. I didn't tell anyone but my close family and best friend because I was ashamed and didn't want anyone to know. I was back at square one – jobless. I couldn't understand. I became angry at God and found it hard to trust Him. How could He let this happen? The enemy plagued my mind with doubt and worry. "Who's going to hire you now?" "You're a new graduate and you got laid off." "No one is going to hire you." "Look at you, you can't even keep a job." All of these thoughts ran through my head as the enemy taunted me. I started the interview process again and one by one they all said no, and I continued to get rejected. I questioned God and His plan because I couldn't see where He was taking me or what He was going to do next.

March came and went and so did April, and I continued to be discouraged as my hope faded. The enemy's voice was so loud that it was hard for me to hear God. But then one day, I heard a still small voice saying, "Listen to the voice of truth. Trust me again." That was all I needed to have my mindset changed. After that day, I became more positive and hopeful and was more intentional about trusting God. Then one day in May, I went to the city to do a Pediatric Advanced Life Support (PALS) class. While on break, I noticed that I had a missed call and checked voicemail on my phone. I listened to the message and it said, "Hi Cassandra, this is John from nursing recruitment at Fortune Medical Center. We have an opening for a position in the NICU. If you are interested, please give us a call back." I looked at the phone and smiled. I knew that this was God. I called my mom and told her, and she was overjoyed. I scheduled the interview and trusted that God's will would be done. This was a job that I hadn't even applied for, but God had opened up the right door for me. All I had to do was trust Him.

I went on the interview and was confident when I met with the nurse manager. I told her my story of being born premature at 28 weeks and only weighing a pound and a couple of ounces. She was amazed and kept saying that I was someone that she needed in her unit to encourage the parents. Everything had come full circle and God had truly answered prayers. The interview went well, and I was offered the job and was set to start on June 5. What a difference six months made. I started my dream job in the neonatal intensive care unit on June 5, 2017, and I was in love. From day one of working there I knew that this was where I belonged. Now, four years later, I am still in love with what I do and with being able to make a difference in the smallest of lives. When one door closed, another one was opened up for me even though I couldn't see it at the time. All it took was me trusting God again. He has proved Himself before and He won't stop now. Even in the most difficult moments, TRUST GOD. He hasn't failed you yet and He won't start now.

www.ingramcontent.com/pod-product-compliance
Lightning Source LLC
Chambersburg PA
CBHW060133100426
42744CB00007B/776

* 9 781954 609105 *